SHAKESPEARE
A CRASH
COURSE

SHAKESPEARE
A CRASH COURSE
ROB GRAHAM

TED SMART

This edition produced in 2003 for
The Book People Ltd,
Hall Wood Avenue, Haydock,
St. Helens WA11 9UL

*This book was conceived, designed
and produced by*
THE IVY PRESS LIMITED
The Old Candlemakers, West Street
Lewes, East Sussex, BN7 2NZ

Creative Director: PETER BRIDGEWATER
Publisher: SOPHIE COLLINS
Editorial Director: STEVE LUCK
Designer: JANE LANAWAY
Editor: GRAPEVINE PUBLISHING SERVICES
DTP Designer: CHRIS LANAWAY
Picture Research: VANESSA FLETCHER
Illustrations: IVAN HISSEY

Printed and bound in China by

Hong Kong Graphics and Printing Ltd.

DEDICATION

For Joe and Erin

Contents

Introduction

This book is about William Shakespeare, alias 'The Bard', a shady character from history about whom

very little is actually known, but who nevertheless remains the most famous and most quoted (and also most misquoted) writer in history. His awesome vocabulary is estimated at approximately 30,000 words (triple that of most people) from which he wove his 38 plays, 4 poems and 154 sonnets. But what a pity he didn't keep a diary too!

And this writing has never been bettered. It is packed with words, images (7,342 to be exact), action, poetry, humour, rhythm, penetrating psychological and philosophical insight, and metaphors that create incredible beauty and power of thought and feelings.

'Remember, I know where you live.'
Laurence Olivier as Richard III making friends, in the 1955 film.

Yet Shakespeare didn't write for posterity; he had to write to please his audience. Hence the mixture of soliloquies, lofty speeches, silly puns, insults and even complete nonsense. He borrowed stories from anywhere and everywhere (and some are frankly silly). His characters can be vulgar, sometimes shocking, and may rant and rave. But he wrote with heart, wit, intelligence, eloquence and style.

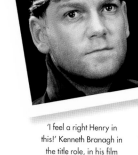

'I feel a right Henry in this!' Kenneth Branagh in the title role, in his film of *Henry V*.

DRAMATIS PERSONAE

The actors, managers, playwrights, characters, lords and commoners who influenced the Bard, or later figures who've taken his name in vain!

The Chandos portrait, attributed to John Taylor.

He took risks. He transformed dull stories and blank verse into the perfect form to carry the speech of ordinary folk as well as that of scholars, priests, aristocrats and philosophers. As with true genius, he turned sows' ears into beautiful silk purses.

The Elizabethan theatre was the perfect stage for Shakespeare. It was an imaginative theatre with no scenery and few props, so everything had to be in the writing

GROUNDLINGS'
GOSSIP

Groundlings were the common-or-garden Elizabethans who stood around in front of the stage to watch the plays because they couldn't afford seats. These boxes give you a hint of what they might have been discussing as they waited for the play to begin.

(in Macbeth, *for example, there are about 40 speeches mentioning or describing locations, times of day and weather conditions). It didn't pretend its audiences weren't there. And they, in turn, demanded of it stories of passion, greatness and evil, fantasy and the supernatural, but stories that also had relevance to the real issues in their short and hard lives. Shakespeare gave them that and more.*

Shakespeare's work has been translated, published, adapted, filmed and televised for almost every country in the world. His name is perhaps the best-known on the planet. The Internet is still in its infancy, yet there are already about half a million web pages – some of them most useful – devoted to his life, his work and related issues.

'Will you cover yourself up, woman! Can't you see we're being watched, or have you gone mad?'

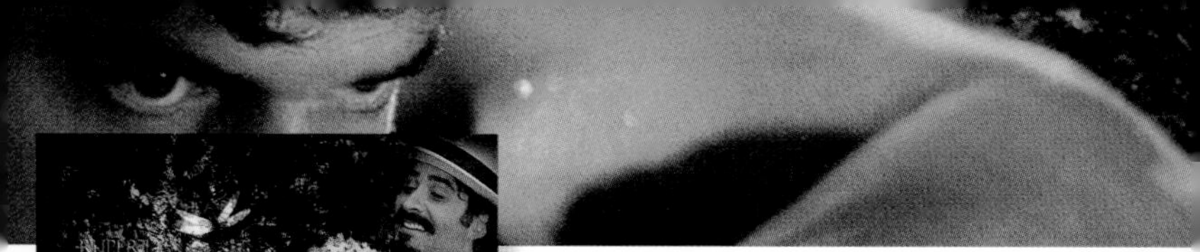

If you go down to
the woods today...

'It'll end in tears...'
Shakespeare
immortalized
once more.

Critics and educators are constantly telling us what art, poetry and dramatic writing really 'mean'; many people spend their lives studying Shakespeare, and most produce valuable work. But really we all should take a few risks, as Shakespeare did, and trust our own instincts about what is good and bad. As Joseph Addison wrote in 1714, it is far better to read Shakespeare 'where there is not a single rule observed', than anything produced by a critic, 'where there is not one of them violated'. So read this little book and then go off and see the plays for yourself.

Rob Graham

Timeline

More of a contextual chronology than a timeline, this is a selected list of major events happening at the time the works were being written and performed (or filmed, televised or otherwise bowdlerized).

Rob Graham

1547 Ivan the Terrible becomes the first Russian ruler to take the title Czar (derived from the Roman 'Caesar').

1550s English traders land in Benin, in search of gold and slaves.

1577 Raphael Holinshed writes *The Chronicles of England, Scotland, and Irelande*, providing source material for a number of Shakespeare's plays.

1547~1598
The Bard in Babylon!
Schoolboys in the chapels of Satan

The London that lured Shakespeare to it some time between 1585 and 1592 wasn't exactly paved with gold. Poor harvests resulted in food riots (indeed, Queen Elizabeth had to impose martial law in 1595). Although England had thrashed the Spanish Armada in 1588, which made everyone feel better (unless they were Spanish), the plague returned a couple of years later to wipe away any smirks. Theatre, however, was in the ascendant, prompting Puritans to call London a 'Babylon of sensuality and excess'. And if that isn't a potent calling to an aspiring young thespian from Stratford, I don't know what is!

'When my agent said I had the lead role, I didn't expect this!' *The Martyrdom of St Apollonia*, an open-air performance.

Morality and mystery plays had been a popular form of entertainment since the 14th century, and, although banned in 1547 during the Reformation, these outdoor communal dramas continued until the 1570s. They were generally presented on horse-drawn carts and performed by tradesmen (the word 'mystery' is an archaic term for a 'trade', not a religious whodunnit

– if you don't believe me just think back to the last time you watched a tradesman at work in your home – what *was* the guy up to for all those hours?). As well as the mystery and morality plays, there were the 'school' plays – written for academic performance with schoolboy actors.

'Right, I'll book the hotel, you get the tickets for the show.' *The Magi*, from a Miracle play.

1581 Sedan chairs come into general use in England.

1582 Leap years are introduced for the first time, but the tradition that ladies can propose on 29 February comes much later.

1583 Galileo Galilei times a swinging chandelier against his pulse in a cathedral in Pisa and figures out that each swing of a pendulum takes the same time regardless of its weight and displacement.

Most famous of these were *Ralph Roister Doister*, a comedy penned in 1550 by Nicholas Udall, and *Gammer Gurton's Needle*, written around 1560 by William Stevenson. In 1561, *Gorboduc*, by Thomas Sackville and Thomas Norton, was first performed for the Queen at the Inner Court. Although dull, it was at least in English and in blank verse (instead of the usual Roman dramas in Latin) and was thus instrumental in establishing the five-act form for tragedy later pursued with such gusto by Shakespeare.

By 1576, private theatres for the upper classes, such as Blackfriars, were flourishing. Here they could watch plays performed by the boys of the Chapel Royal Choir. The same year James Burbage built an open-air public playhouse, the Theatre, outside the city walls at Shoreditch (since the Puritans and the elders of London wouldn't allow such a 'chapel of Satan' within). The fabric of the building was

DRAMATIS PERSONAE

Professional actors were gaining respectability during the 16th century, often enjoying royal or noble patronage, which they needed to protect them from political or religious attack (Henry VIII had eight players under his care). So, fortunately for Shakespeare, by the time he came to London there were theatres and sponsors eager for new talent, and ready and waiting to hire him.

James Burbage's Theatre showing the simplicity of the staging

GROUNDLINGS' GOSSIP

In his essay 'Of Masques and Triumphs', Francis Bacon described how stage managers would create special effects by using particular colours on stage – 'white, carnation and sea-water green', for example, showed up best in candlelight. He also recalls the characters of a masque as 'fools, satyrs, baboons, wild men, sprites, witches and pigmies'.

removed to the Bankside in December 1598, where it was set up as the Globe. With the Theatre, the first permanent public buildings specially intended for plays had come into being. It was to these that young Will went to work as actor and writer. The rest, as they say, is history.

1558 The first doll's house is built, in Germany.

1576 Military leader Oda Nobunaga builds a Japanese moated fortress at Azuchi.

1586 A 75-ton obelisk is erected in Rome's St Peter's Square. It requires 907 men and 75 horses to move it 320 m (800 ft) from the Circus of Nero.

1547~1600

The Elizabethan Funzone

Festivals, frolics and frivolity

All was fun and jollification at the end of the 16th century – if you'd managed to escape the plague, that is. Most festivals in Tudor times were for everyone – 'class distinctions' in the modern sense had no place here. Although there were different economic groups, the English people still identified with a largely common culture (and have been nostalgic for it ever since).

Enough to put the wind up you

Among the more exotic features of popular festivals were the 'mystical bestiary', and 'blasts of air' (signifying the presence of spirits). So the customary consumption of flatulent foods on Shrove Tuesday has a cosmic connection with the supernatural belief in returning souls after all ('Ooops! Pardon me... I could swear that was Great Uncle Fred!')

Elizabeth I enjoying some courtly frolics (oh, those wild, wild Royals).

There were three main types of communal festivity, and it is likely that Shakespeare would have frequently made his presence felt at all of them (performing at most and getting drunk at the rest). He certainly referred to them in many of his plays. The 'popular' festivals, rooted in traditions such as folksong and story-telling, mystery plays and farces, and the great seasonal celebrations such as Christmas, New Year, Carnival, May and Midsummer, were full of merry-making, rude songs, stories and satirical poems; and those who laughed the most, according to one commentator, were 'children, women and the common people'. Ribald stories would throw into sharp relief the hard facts of life. In fact the whole affair encapsulated what we latter-day clever-clogs have come to term the 'carnivalesque', as defined by the 20th-century critic Mikhail Bakhtin: turning the world upside down (parody), preoccupying

1590 The Great Bed of Ware, an enormous bed almost 3.6m (12 ft) square is installed in Hertfordshire, largely as a tourist attraction.

1592 Robert Greene publishes his pamphlet 'A Quip for an Upstart Courtier'. He dies later in the year, of overindulgence.

1593 Playwright Christopher Marlowe dies violently in mysterious circumstances in a Deptford tavern.

itself with the material and the physical (bodily functions), and embracing opposites and contradictions (life/death, etc. etc.). Even then the clown/jester/fool had a cutting edge, a sinister side, a sombre depth to his character. Brush up your Shakespeare and you'll see.

As well as the popular festivals, there were the 'pageants': spectacular processions consisting of mobile 'stages' – platforms or wagons. The word 'pageant' was originally used to describe the mystery plays performed at the Corpus Christi festival, celebrated the Thursday after Pentecost. In 1547, however, during the Reformation, the Corpus Christi guilds were dissolved. But the ever-popular pageants continued, even as Elizabeth I slyly brought in the Protestant calendar (she was no fool). They eventually became secularized and became part of the Lord Mayor's shows.

DRAMATIS PERSONAE

The ruling classes were always moaning that popular festivities encouraged disrespect for orthodox religion. Records of clerical trials at the time tell of members of the congregation breaking out into spontaneous morris-dancing during sermons, laughing loudly and cutting capers around the church and, in one instance, of a woman coming to church dressed as a man!

Finally there were the royal festivities, mainly with the aristocracy in attendance. These accompanied a coronation, or the seasonal observations of the court that took place in winter (the 'Season of Revels' – *see page 44*), and summer. Tournaments were also popular, as were Christmas entertainments and lovely big summer festivals at stately country homes with fireworks, water pageants and masques. In those days they knew how to have a good time.

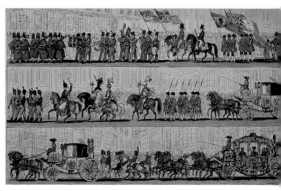

A procession of the Lord Mayor's Show in a multi-storey car park.

GROUNDLINGS' GOSSIP

The Puritans tried to ban festivals (as well as sex, laughter and anything else that betrayed a pulse). One poor bishop by the name of Latimer arrived at a church to preach in April 1549 to find the place locked. His 'flock' had decided they would rather attend a local knees-up in honour of Robin Hood than listen to him droning on about doom and gloom.

1501 In Prague, the first printed hymn book is compiled by Severin, containing 89 Czech hymns.

1519 Ferdinand Magellan sets out with five ships on his expedition to reach the East Indies via the West. He dies, but one of the ships manages the first circumnavigation of the globe.

1598 The English scientist and essayist Francis Bacon is arrested for debt.

1500~1616

So Who Was William Shakespeare?
And why aren't there any photographs?

Shakespeares were dotted all over central England, especially Warwickshire. Richard Shakespeare, who was probably William's grandfather, moved near Stratford in about 1528. He died in 1560 leaving two sons, Harry and John, and some money. Uncle Harry was a bit of a rascal, getting fined in 1574 for fighting in a pub, and again in 1596 for not helping to mend the road!

Hilliard's portrait of Shakespeare, from 1588.

But John was more stable. He became a whittawer, earning a living by making leather goods. In 1558 he married Mary Arden, from a nearby parish, and they had a total of seven children, of whom William was the third. The young Bard was born in Henley Street, Stratford-upon-Avon, Warwickshire, in April 1564, surviving the plague that hit Stratford a few months later. The Warwickshire countryside in which he grew up left indelible images in his mind, which were to re-emerge in the references to flowers, plants and country practices in the plays.

William was educated at the King's New School in Stratford (Stratford Grammar School), built for the sons of local gentry. Certainly he didn't go to university. At school he would have learnt Latin grammar and read the Roman as well as Greek classics (which included *Aesop's*

Shakespeare's birthplace, at Henley Street, Stratford-upon-Avon.

1600 An inventory of Elizabeth I's wardrobe includes 102 French gowns, 99 robes and 125 petticoats.

1607 King James' plans to unite the kingdoms of England and Scotland fail.

1616 Walter Raleigh, imprisoned for treason in the Tower of London, is released on parole to search for El Dorado.

> ### GROUNDLINGS' GOSSIP
>
> Shakespeare died on 23 April (St George's Day) 1616. Because he was baptized in Stratford's Holy Trinity Church on 26 April 1564, and because it was usual for baptism to take place just a few days after birth, it is assumed he must have been born on 23 April as well. Spooky!

Fables, and plays by Seneca, Terence and Plautus just waiting to be turned into something interesting). It isn't known how long he attended, but the actor *Thomas BETTERTON* (1634–1710), who researched Shakespeare's life, claimed that John Shakespeare withdrew William around 1577 to be apprenticed to his leather business when his fortunes were sliding.

When William was born, his father was fairly successful. However, 13 years later, his business was failing. He had risen in local government council to high bailiff, but when things went downhill, he was sacked as alderman for not doing his job. In 1592, while young Will was annoying Robert Greene as an 'upstart crow' in London, his poor old dad wouldn't even go to church for fear of meeting debt collectors. For the next nine years, until he died in 1601, John was subsidized by his son. Perhaps it was seeing his old man make such a dog's dinner of things that prompted William's later business successes?

'I must do something about getting the chimney swept.' The genius of Shakespeare illustrated in a comic, *Hobbes*, which was published in 1888.

DRAMATIS PERSONAE

John Shakespeare applied for a coat of arms in 1576, but was turned down, for he was beset by trouble. He mortgaged what he owned, fell into debt with relatives and others and collected personal enemies who intimidated him to such an extent that, in 1582, he petitioned against them 'for fear of death and mutilation of his limbs'. *William later acquired the coat of arms for him.*

1568 Flemish scientist/cartographer Gerardius Mercator devises an improved mapping system that allows more accurate navigation.

1577 Francis Drake makes his first journey around the world in the *Pelican*.

1589 Thomas Kyd writes the *Spanish Tragedy*, the first of the revenge tragedies.

1556~1652
She Was Only the Farmer's Daughter...
The Shakespeares and the Hathaways

Anne Hathaway was probably the eldest daughter of farmer Richard Hathaway, who rented Hewlands Farm (now 'Anne Hathaway's Cottage') from the Earl of Warwick. In his will Richard left 10 marks to his daughter 'Agnes', who was probably Anne (the names were then interchangeable), and died before she married. Of Anne we know almost nothing, for she was born before births were entered in Stratford parish registers. But according to her gravestone she was 67 when she died in 1623, which means she was about eight years older than Shakespeare.

Hewlands Farm, alias Anne Hathaway's Cottage, at sunset. One wonders whether Shakespeare would have seen it with such rose-tinted glasses.

In September 1582, the 18-year-old Will met Anne Hathaway, probably in one of those fields he was forever wandering about in, because by November she was three months pregnant. They had to marry – as one did in those days; no Family Planning counselling or social welfare then; the Church had a

The older woman
A description of Anne Hathaway depicts a 'powerful, even attractively masculine woman, eight years older than the writer, one capable of obsessing her young husband for many miserable, jealous years, then of maddening and amusing and at last boring him.' If this is an accurate picture, it does much to explain William's flight to London!

serious grip on such issues (if you'll forgive the pun). It was Lent, when marriages could not be solemnized, so they had to apply for a special licence at a court in Worcester.

In 1583 their daughter Susanna was born, and was baptized on 16 May. Two years later, Anne had the

1604 *The Honest Whore, Part I*, by Thomas Dekker and Thomas Middleton, is performed by the Children of St Paul's Players.

1617 Japan's Yoshiwara prostitute section is established at Edo, after a local vicelord persuades the authorities to license him to operate brothels in exchange for surveillance of suspicious strangers.

1649 In England, the Commonwealth is established under Puritan Oliver Cromwell.

GROUNDLINGS' GOSSIP

Shakespeare's twin children were named, it is thought, after some friends of his, the local baker and his wife Hamnet and Judith Sadler. Hamnet Sadler then named one of his children Will, in 1598, and in 1616 he witnessed the dying Shakespeare's will. Hamnet was remembered in the will, but I wonder if Will remembered young Will in his will.

---

twins, Judith and Hamnet, baptized on 2 February 1585. Hamnet died of unknown causes in 1596 (alas, poor Hamnet, he wasn't well…). Although there is no proof that Willy and Anne did not get on too well, when he left for London in 1592, he left alone, and there is no record of him ever asking her to London to stay with him. Perhaps it was with her in mind that he later wrote in *Twelfth Night*, '*Then let thy love be younger than thyself… For women are as roses, whose fair flow'r being once displayed doth fall that very hour*'. Or even, '*Crabbed age and youth cannot live together; youth is full of pleasance, age is full of care.*' (from his poem *The Passionate Pilgrim*).

Their first child, Susanna (William's favourite) married John Hall, a physician, in 1607. She was a witty woman and could read and write. She was also a bit of a rebel. In 1606, along with 20 other people, she was accused of failing to receive Communion one Easter Sunday. Following the Gunpowder Plot in 1605, anyone believed to have Catholic leanings was in danger, so the charge was serious. However, Susanna was acquitted, and her name was cleared.

Susanna's younger sister Judith remained illiterate and her wits completely failed her when she married, at what was then considered the 'advanced' age of 31, Thomas Quiney (son of Richard who was a bailiff and friend of Shakespeare). Thomas opened a tobacco and wine shop and proceeded to sell adulterated wines, for which he was fined. He abandoned Judith in 1652, and there is nothing that would suggest he ever returned to her.

'I have to go to London, Anne. I'll only be gone a short while.'

1597 English barrister-scientist Francis Bacon publishes his 'Essays' in which he says: 'Some books are to be tasted, others to be swallowed, and some few to be chewed and digested'.

1598 Thomas Bodley begins rebuilding a library at Oxford (it will be known as the Bodleian).

1636 Harvard, the first North American university, is founded.

1550~the present

Yes, But Was He Who He Said He Was?

Or was he the Earl of Oxford, or Francis Bacon, or Elvis?

One of the great controversies surrounding the plays and poems is their authorship – some contend that Shakespeare didn't really write all those plays and sonnets at all; Someone Else did. And the identity of that Someone Else? As you'd expect, there have been several nominations.

Edward de Vere. Could this man have written *King Lear*?

The chief suspect is Edward de Vere, 17th Earl of Oxford (1550–1604). Sigmund Freud supported him, writing in 1930: 'I no longer believe in the man from Stratford'; but then Freud didn't believe anything unless someone's mother was involved. De Vere's fans claimed he had the money, breeding, education and general 'upper-classness' to have made him a genius, seeming to overlook the fact that such a recipe has, in the past, had more to do with producing inbred idiots than

Looney tunes

In 1918, a man left a sealed envelope with the British Museum. In it, he said, was proof that Edward de Vere really wrote Will's plays and poems. He had already sent a manuscript detailing this 'proof' to a publisher, who rejected it unless he changed his name. The man refused. Another publisher took it on, and, in 1920, *Shakespeare Identified* appeared, by... J. Thomas Looney.

genii. Besides, Ben Jonson was the son of a bricklayer who never went to university... so who wrote his plays, eh? The debate goes something like this: 'Stratford-upon-Avon', cry Oxfordians, 'was a backwater full of country bumpkins who couldn't have written something as wonderful as *Hamlet*, never mind *Shakespeare: A Crash Course*.' 'Rubbish!' sneer Will's Men,

1739 Celebrated English highwayman Dick Turpin is hanged in York, bowing to the ladies present before leaping from the scaffold.

1856 William Henry Perkins makes the first synthetic dye, a discovery made by accident while working as an assistant at the Royal College of Chemistry in London.

1969 *Monty Python's Flying Circus* premieres on British television.

'What about the fact that De Vere died in 1604, huh, when only two-thirds of the plays had been written?' 'Ha!' stabs the rapier-like retort of sheer genius, 'that's because the dates for the plays are, er, wrong. They have been changed... by you lot!' It's Montagues and Capulets all over again. Interestingly, if Oxford did write the plays, why didn't he acknowledge the fact? His supporters say that since some of them contain political 'criticism' he didn't dare, so he used the name 'Shakespeare' instead. This has to be one of the weakest arguments ever mounted.

> ### GROUNDLINGS' GOSSIP
>
> Others nominated for the title of True Author have been Sir Francis Bacon, championed by several (including Mark Twain), but support for Bacon fell out of fashion in the 1920s. Then there was Christopher Marlowe, but he died in 1593 at the age of 29, so if it was he, well... he must have been a very busy boy is all I can say!

Sir Francis Bacon gives an interview to the local press about his next play.

'I'm giving up acting to join a band.'

However, it is likely that others penned at least some parts of some of the plays. For example, three song and dance passages in *Macbeth*, some scenes in *Henry VIII* (possibly by John Fletcher) and the first two acts of *Pericles* were probably not Shakespeare's work. Why this should be so, though, is a mystery. Perhaps when Will grew fed up with a certain passage not working out he bought someone a drink in the pub to sort it out. But we'll never know, for as Hamlet put it, 'The rest is silence'.

1621 The first Thanksgiving Day is celebrated by Puritans thanking God for their first year in America.

1753 British man Jonas Hanway carries a parasol as protection from the rain and becomes the first person to use an 'umbrella'.

1821 John Constable completes his painting *Landscape, Noon* (later renamed *The Hay Wain*).

1616~the present

A Load of Old Bardolatry
I was lost, but then I found Shakespeare

The word 'Bardolatry' was coined by the irascible George Bernard Shaw in 1901 to describe the worship of all things Shakespearean. Bardolatry began innocently in 1623, when John Heminges and Henry Condell, actor friends of Shakespeare, collected 36 of his plays, supplemented them with eulogies – most notably an especially glowing one by Ben Jonson – and published them as the 'First Folio'. They had no idea just what a giant industry they were spawning with this act of homage to their friend.

The title page of the First Folio Edition.

Jubilee Procession campaigners in Stratford on a 'Stamp out Bardolatry' march.

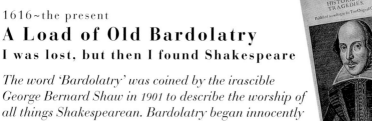

Bardolatry became evangelical when David Garrick held a Stratford Jubilee in 1769, although Stratford had attracted tourists prior to this, who came to see such icons as the mulberry tree thought to have been planted by Shakespeare in the garden of his home, New Place. They came in sufficient numbers as to properly annoy the then owner William Gastrell – so much so that he chopped the tree down, and in 1759 demolished the whole house! Then Shakespeare's birthplace in Henley Street (known by Bardolaters as the 'Birthplace') also joined the list of hallowed high spots,

1877 Edward S. Morse, zoology teacher at Tokyo University, gives the first lecture in Japan on Darwinian theory to an enthusiastic audience.

1901 Scot Hubert Booth invents the first electrical vacuum cleaner, but unable to afford to promote it, he sells the rights to relative William Hoover.

1970 Peter Brook's ground-breaking production of *A Midsummer Night's Dream* opens in London.

as did Anne Hathaway's Cottage and Mary Arden's House. During the late 18th century, the Henley Street house became an inn, and thus was able to offer, as Ivor Brown has noted, Bed, Board and Bard.

In America, Shakespeare dominated early theatre repertoire. A *Richard III* by *Colley CIBBER* (1671–1757) successfully opened the theatre season in New York. But elsewhere the Puritans were busy with their ethic cleansing; they persuaded, for example, the Commonwealth of Massachusetts to pass a law banning all theatrical performances because of their 'painted vanities'. And in New England *Othello* was billed as 'A Series of Moral Dialogues, in Five Parts, Depicting the Evils of Jealousy and Other Bad Passions', which may be accurate, but hardly very

> ### GROUNDLINGS' GOSSIP
>
> Although Widow Hornby, a tenant of the Birthplace, sold pieces of a chair said to be 'Shakespeare's own', strangely enough, the original never seemed to get any smaller. The owner of the house, another widow, evicted Hornby to steal the Bard-industry for herself. But Hornby moved across the road, with her chair and other relics, and the widows hurled abuse at each other ever after.

sophisticated. Happily not everywhere was so uncivilized. In 1773–74, 13 of the plays were performed in South Carolina alone. Bardolatry grew in America.

In 1840 the Shakespeare Society was formed in England, and branches opened across Europe and America, many of which are thriving today. In 1936, by request, dust from the Birthplace garden was put in a box made from charred wood from the ruins of the 1926 Shakespeare Memorial Theatre. This 'sacred earth' and 'holy water' (from the Avon) were then taken to consecrate the new Shakespeare Theatre in Dallas, Texas!

Colley Cibber as Lord Foppington, his own creation.

Boring Bard

From about 1858, Bardolatry spread through English school curricula. But the idea of considering Shakespeare's work from a dramatic point of view didn't penetrate academia until very recently. For most of the time his dramas were buried in 'literature' departments – the morgue attendants of art. As Ivor Brown said in his *Shakespeare* (1949), 'Like most schoolboys, I had been sickened of Shakespeare by education'.

1585 Kronborg Castle is completed at Elsinore (Helsingör) for Denmark's Frederick II on the site of an earlier castle.

1586 Scientist Simon Stevin outlines the mathematical proof that two unequal weights fall through the same distance in the same time.

1587 Mary, Queen of Scots, is executed at Fotheringay Castle after nearly 19 years in prison.

1585~1592

Wild Bill and the Lost Years
Was he poaching, praying or abducted by aliens?

From 1585 until 1592, Shakespeare seemed to disappear. That's to say there is no record of his whereabouts or activities. And for nearly 400 years we have worried about the lad. Where on earth could he have been, and just what was he up to? This period of Shakespeare's life has become known as the 'lost years'.

GROUNDLINGS' GOSSIP

Perhaps the most well-known yarn regarding Shakespeare's alcoholic pursuits is the 'crab-apple tree' story, dubious though it is. Apparently Shakespeare visited the village of Bideford planning to compete with the local hard drinkers only to find they were away drinking elsewhere, so he was forced to spend the night (presumably stone-cold *and* sober) under a crab-apple tree.

Even before the 'disappearance', we know little about his activities after he left school. One rather exciting story has it that he was a bit of a tearaway and took to poaching deer and rabbits from a Warwickshire squire, Sir Thomas Lucy, who according to a local clergyman '…oft had him whipped and sometimes imprisoned' for it. So young Will ran away. The story gets better, with several claims that Shakespeare revenged himself on Sir Lucy by portraying him as Justice Shallow in *The Merry Wives of Windsor*. It has been pointed out, however, that Lucy was not the same stupid bachelor as Justice Shallow, and that it had after all been 14 years between the 'poaching' incident and *The Merry Wives of Windsor*. Then there's the 'great drinker' stories. A good one tells of his debt to a wine merchant who offered

'Yes, yes, I am Justice Shallow, I am he. But I just don't care what story you say you are following up. I've never heard of this man Shakespeare, I tell you!'

1587 Christopher Marlowe writes *Tamburlaine the Great*, marking the beginning of the golden age of Elizabethan and Jacobean drama in England.

1590 Italian artist Caravaggio paints *The Cardsharp*.

1591 Japanese tea-master Rikyu Sen commits ritual suicide (*seppuku*) on orders from Toyotomi Hideyoshi, the imperial regent.

to cancel it if Shakespeare could cleverly answer four questions: what pleased God best, what pleased the devil best, what pleased the world best and what pleased him best? Shakespeare at once replied:

> 'God is best pleas'd when men discard their sin
> Satan's best pleas'd when they persist therein
> The world's best pleas'd when you do sell good wine
> And you're best pleas'd when I do pay for mine.'

Needless to say, Shakespeare's debt was written off at once!

Another tale claims that he spent his lost years at a Catholic retreat, and since Catholicism was punishable by death, he thought it wise to keep it secret. He might also have been a schoolmaster in

Hamlet's guests, the players, discuss 'The Mouse-trap' over a couple of pints.

Warwickshire or even toured as an apprentice actor with one of the growing number of provincial theatre companies. When, in 1592, Robert Greene nastily described Shakespeare as the 'upstart crow, beautified with our feathers' it was long assumed he was alluding to a newcomer to the stage, but since Shakespeare was 28 this seems unlikely. Besides, the *Henry VI* plays appeared from about 1590, suggesting he had been involved with theatre for some time by then.

Will Hood

Other stories of his antics during the 'lost years' have him stealing deer to furnish his wedding feast, and seducing the gamekeeper's daughter in the process. Or present him as a sort of Robin Hood character (very popular then) who was fighting to maintain the rights of forest traditions and trapping game. As such, it is said that he was whipped and put in the stocks.

'Hello, Small Person! I'm William Shakespeare. Do you want my autograph?'

'Never heard of you, baldy. And anyway, what's an autograph?'

1603 In Japan a female attendant of the Izumo shrine leads a performance on a dry river bed, which includes dancing and comic sketches, and comes to be known as 'kabuki' theatre.

1650 Mathematicians are by now using the signs +, -, ×, ÷, = and √.

1780 The Derby horse-race is held for the first time in Britain.

1594~1910
Foul Papers and Folios
From random scribblings to collected works

Shakespeare was a pragmatic working actor/writer for a robust and popular theatre that had a huge appetite for novelty. Plays were rotated in theatres every two or three days. Typically a writer produced an outline plot (known as 'foul papers'), sometimes in collaboration, for his colleagues to approve, whereupon it became the property of the company.

Who gets the biggest part?

DRAMATIS PERSONAE

The cowardly Falstaff, *who appeared in* Henry IV *and* Henry VI, *but not in* Henry V *(he ran away and wouldn't fight), was probably originally called 'Oldcastle' after Sir John Oldcastle, but his family thought this a slur. It has been suggested that Elizabeth I intervened and 'was pleas'd to command [Shakespeare] to alter it'.*

A log having to support Falstaff.

Whether it saw the light of day was not just dependent upon the quality of the writing but also upon those old familiar factors: fashion, commercial viability, the limitations of the space for performance and the actors' needs (usually for the biggest part). When everyone was happy, scribes made two more copies. One of these was kept as a prompt book on which a 'stage manager' scribbled notes concerning props, costumes etc. (and would even censor bits if he judged it necessary). Thus the play in performance might diverge considerably from the original.

About half of Shakespeare's plays appeared individually in cheap 'quarto' volumes between 1594 and 1622, mostly from his own drafts (often identified as

1815 The Prince Regent, son of George III, engages architect John Nash to remodel the notorious Pavilion in Brighton, England.

1837 Charles Dickens' novel *Oliver Twist* is published in England.

1900 In New York H.J. Heinz erects an electric sign six storeys high to tell New Yorkers about his '57 Good Things for the Table', including tomato soup, ketchup and pickles.

such by his peculiar spellings). But there were some 'bad quartos' put together from the dodgy recollections of second-rate actors for second-rate printers keen to cash in on a stage hit. Happily these were replaced by versions released by Shakespeare's theatre company, which were ultimately collected together (minus *Pericles*) in the 1623 Folio edition entitled *Mr William Shakespears Comedies, Histories & Tragedies*.

Several editions followed in the 18th and 19th centuries, and in 1910 Methuen published a facsimile edition of the four folios. Since then thousands of printings of the *Collected Works*, as well as individual plays, have been published, in more than 70 languages.

Dramatic origami

A 'quarto' was a sheet of paper folded twice – that is four leaves, and eight pages. A 'folio', however, was a large sheet of paper printed on both sides and then folded once to make two leaves and thus just four pages. So, the printed books became known by the size of the pages in them. Simple, huh?

'Of course we're your friends, Caesar! Don't you trust us?'

GENIUS DEFINED?

'Greatness' is difficult to pin down, but one reason Shakespeare was 'great' was because he bound new blank verse, old classic rhyme and prose together in varying amounts appropriate to the subject and tone of each play (so while *Julius Caesar* is mostly blank verse with little prose, *The Merry Wives of Windsor* is just the opposite). He took old stories and remodelled them into superb dramas using unparalleled imagery and penetrating insight. Jonson came close when he said his greatness was to do with the 'dimensions of his soul', which were vast indeed.

For Bardophiles

One thousand copies of the Folio collection (containing over 900 pages) were sold in 1623. One was given to Augustine Vincent, as per the instructions of printer William Jaggard, who died four days before the collection was registered; one went to the Bodleian Library. Records show only about 240 remain in existence today, and only a dozen of those in perfect condition. So if you see one – snap it up!

Mrs Page seems to be having a few local difficulties in Windsor.

1572 Thousands of Huguenots are killed in the St Bartholomew's Day massacre in Paris, at Catherine de' Medici's instigation.

1580 Wu Ch'eng-en, author of the classic Chinese picaresque novel *Monkey*, dies.

1590 Dutch scientist Zacharian Janssen invents the microscope.

1564~1616

Shexpere's Spelyng Lesen

Or, what I wouldn't give for a spel-checka

The conveyancing paper for Blackfriars House showing Will's only known signature.

What's in a name, you ask? Well, mock ye not, ye churlish canker-clawed clapper-blossoms, because in Shakespeare's case the answer's an awful lot! In fact you've no idea *how much heated argument this subject has caused among academics and writers over the years. This is largely because some of them, usually supporters of the Oxford or Bacon theory (see page 16) have suggested that the various spellings prove he didn't write any plays at all and that 'William Shakespeare', London poet and playwright, was a different chap to 'William Shaksper', glover's son from Stratford.*

Indeed, it's true that Shakespeare did seem to have trouble spelling his name the same way twice, although he was well enough educated. And whatever the reason, the 20 or so different spellings that have been spotted do seem rather excessive. Some of them are quite inventive, however. 'Shakespeare' was used most of all, but there was 'Shakespear' (spot the difference), 'Shake-speare', 'Shexpere', 'Shagspere' (one for Austin Powers there – 'ShagaBardic, Baby!'), 'Schakespe' and shortest of all, 'Shakp', which sounds a lot like what someone with a mouthful of tough mutton and wine might have coughed.

Most scholars now conclude that one reason for such variety in Elizabethan spelling was general illiteracy. Despite having some rules of grammar, spelling in those days was habitually erratic, often within the same document. If someone liked hyphens, for example, they appeared

---

GROUNDLINGS' GOSSIP

Within William Camden's book *Remaines of a Greater Worke, Concerning Britaine* (1605), is a section devoted to the origins of names. He claims that many names were derived from the equipment of soldiers returning from the Crusades. Thus there were Long-swords, Broad-spears and Breake-speares. It is possible, then, that Shakespeare's ancestors were so named as an abbreviation for 'He-that-has-had-a-Bad-Fright'?

1604 James I of England publishes his 'Counterblaste to Tobacco' describing smoking as 'vile', 'stinking' and 'dangerous'.

1610 English historian and cartographer John Speed begins work on his publication *Theatre of the Empire of Great Britain* – a series of 54 maps of different areas of England and Wales.

1616 Beaumont and Fletcher write the play *The Scornful Lady*, containing the line 'Beggars must be no choosers', derived from a proverb.

all over the place. In London the standard and consistency of grammar was higher than in rural areas (where anyone who could utter 'SHEEP', 'TURNIPS' and 'GERROFFMYLAND!' was reckoned to have an awesome vocabulary). Thus 'Shakespeare' was the preferred version in London, while any of the others would do in the country. A second reason was the difference between spelling in printed and handwritten texts. Early printing compositors developed the habit of spelling any repeated word the same way, which is understandable and such good discipline it was carried on until fairly recently. But handwriting was all over the place. The actor Edward Alleyne bought some sonnets titled, in print, 'Shakespeares Sonnets' but wrote in his notebook that they were 'Shaksper sonetts'. This sort of thing was common. Christopher Marlowe was baptized 'Marlow', yet

Mad, bad and dangerous to know: OK, so Marlowe was a forger, spy, violent drunkard and blasphemer, but he also wrote some marvellous plays.

Now let's see… S-H-A-K-S-P-E… no there's another E in there somewhere. Isn't there?

signed his only known signature 'Marley'. The theatre owner Philip Henslowe, in the 1587 deed of business partnership with John Cholmley, spelled his name 'Henslow', 'Hinshley' and 'Hinshleye' at subsequent points in the documentation. Of course, this could easily be explained if you picture them drinking to future success as they wrote it.

1595 The Ottoman sultan Murad III dies aged 49 after a 21-year reign of debauchery in which he has sired 102 children.

1596 A practical water closet invented by English poet Sir John Harington has few buyers and the privy and chamber pot remain in common use for centuries.

1609 Galileo develops an astronomical telescope and observes craters on the Moon.

1592~1616

Bill and Ben the Drinking Men
Shakespeare and Jonson hit town

'Which pub is this, Will?' 'What's in a name? It's what's in your glass that counts!'

Depending on who you read, Ben JONSON (1572–1637) was either Shakespeare's great friend and drinking partner, or his great rival and enemy. Stories supporting the first school of thought portray the poets as a pair of talented rascals boozing together in the Greyhound in Stratford or the Three Pigeons in Brentford; and the Falcon Tavern on Bankside claims Shakespeare, Jonson and their mates drank there daily (and there's a pub near me where Elvis drinks every other Tuesday...). The other camp claims that Jonson felt considerable antagonism towards Shakespeare, and cites as evidence the well-known comment he made in his otherwise respectful eulogy about Shakespeare's limited grasp of Greek and Latin.

Additionally, fairly groundless stories have sprung up over the years telling of the verbal and literary sparring between the two men. One example is by Thomas Fuller, who fancifully describes them in his *History of The Worthies of England* (1662) as being like a battle between a 'Spanish galleon [Jonson] and an English man-of-war [Shakespeare]' where 'Jonson was built far higher in learning' but was 'slow, in his performances' whereas Shakespeare was 'lighter in sailing, could turn... by the quickness of his wit and invention'.

The biographer Nicholas Rowe, in his *Works* (1709), even has the Bard give Ben Jonson his first theatre commission! This story has it that an unknown Jonson had a play turned down by a theatre. Shakespeare heroically intervened and 'found something so well in it as to... read

1610 *Peribanez* by Lope de Vega is performed in Spain, depicting 15th-century peasants driven to murder their tyrannical lord in defence of their honour.

1615 English architect Inigo Jones accepts an appointment as surveyor-general of the royal buildings.

1616 On Lord Mayor's Day in London, a pageant devised by John Munday features boats, crowned dolphins and frolicking mermaids and mermen.

it through'. After this, claims Rowe, they became firm friends! The story seems difficult to substantiate. Shakespeare certainly acted in Jonson's first play, *Every Man in his Humour* (1598), for the Lord Chamberlain's company, but whether he had the authority to overrule the company's rejection of the text is debatable.

A spectacular little number for a masque by Inigo Jones.

> **DRAMATIS PERSONAE**
>
> In George Stevens' Shakespeare *(1778)* you'll find a story that hinges on Shakespeare's phrase 'All the world's a stage'. He claims Jonson wrote, 'If but stage actors all the world displays,/ Where shall we find spectators of their plays?' To which Shakespeare answered, 'Little, or much, of what we see, we do; / We're all both actors and spectators too.'

Oddly enough, Jonson's death in 1637 inspired greater homage from other writers and notables than had Shakespeare's. Jonson had an entire volume of eulogy written for him, whereas Shakespeare had to wait seven years after his death for his, which must have proved most irksome for the Bard. Jonson, however, not normally given to praising anybody, wrote in that First Folio a most moving tribute to his old rival, containing the immortal lines:

He was not of an age, but for all time!

Mixed masques

Jonson's most famous plays are *Every Man in His Humour* (1598), *Volpone* (1605), *The Alchemist* (1610) and *Bartholomew Fair* (1614). Some of his best writing, though, can be found in the masques he created with Inigo Jones (1573–1652). But the two fell out in 1634 over that burning question – whether the masque should foreground spectacular display or be a dramatic poem based upon classical scholarship. Always a tricky one, that.

1593 Spain's Escorial Palace, by architect Juan Bautista de Toledo, is completed near Madrid after 30 years of construction and includes a church, monastery and mausoleum.

1595 The Dutch East India Company sends its first ships to Asia, and the Dutch build their first settlements on Africa's Guinea coast.

1598 Spain's new king, Philip III, offers a prize of 1,000 crowns for anyone who can discover a method of ascertaining longitude while Holland's Staats-General offers a prize of 10,000 florins.

1592~1616

William the Conqueror
Drinking, lusting, fighting and poetry

If Shakespeare only began a theatrical career in 1592, when records of his life recommence, he must have made quick progress! For as early as 1595 he is listed, along with two others, as a 'payee' for performances of comedies and interludes for Queen Elizabeth herself.

Shakespeare checking the sales ledger: 'So that's 20 quid you owe me.'

Richard Burbage may have been a little slow as a lover, but he was one of the best, and best-known, actors of Shakespearean drama. The son of James, who built the Theatre, he played Richard III, Hamlet, Othello and Lear. Another friend, Edward Alleyne, was a more demonstrative actor than Burbage and seemed better suited to Christopher Marlowe's villain-heroes. *MARLOWE* (1564–93) had been at Cambridge with *Robert GREENE* (1558–92). In

Among his great friends was *Richard BURBAGE* (1567–1619). One story has it that while Burbage was playing Richard III at the Globe, a woman admirer sent a request that he visit her that night, 'under the name of Richard III'. Shakespeare overheard, arrived at her darkened room before Burbage, and took his place, as it were. When her servant announced that 'Richard III' was at the door, Shakespeare roared, 'Too late! William the Conqueror came before Richard III'. Wouldn't it be great if we knew it were true?

Edward II and his manicurist. (Steve Waddinton and Andrew Tiernan in a 1991 production.)

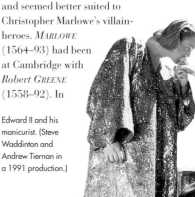

1611 English poet John Donne anonymously publishes 'The Anatomy of the World', an elegy to the late daughter of his patron Sir Robert Drury of Hawsted.

1614 Lope de Vega writes *Fuenteovejuna*, marking a Spanish renaissance in drama.

1615 Firewood becomes increasingly expensive and cheap coal is substituted for the first time.

1589, he was involved in a street fight that left the son of a pub landlord dead. Marlowe was thrown into Newgate prison, but was pardoned by the Queen. However, in 1593 at the Dame Eleanor Bull pub in Deptford, he got into his last fight, and, at the age of 29, was stabbed to death. Fighting and drinking apart, Marlowe left us some wonderful plays: *Tamburlaine the Great* (1587), *The Jew of Malta* (1589), *Edward II* (1592) and *Doctor Faustus* (1604).

Robert Greene was an educated playwright, poet and pamphleteer who preferred a life of dissolution. He was one of the University Wits (now *there's* a contradiction in terms). One of his works, *Pandosto* (1588) was the source of Shakespeare's *The Winter's Tale*. His plays are now forgotten, but not his pamphlets, which attacked everything and everyone. The most famous is in *Greene's Groatsworth of Wit*, in which he calls Shakespeare the 'upstart crow' from a passage that attacks the whole acting profession for being 'Puppets... that spake from our mouths'. His reference is the earliest record we have of Will in London; Greene died that same year.

Greene with envy

Greene may have had good reason to be jealous of Shakespeare. By 1592, the biographer Henry Chettle had commended the Bard as 'excellent in the quality he professes... in writing that proves his art'. Apparently Shakespeare wrote 100,000 dramatic lines, at least 1,000 of them 'perfect'.

Tamburlaine (Anthony Sher) about to make a policy decision.

1568 In Spain El Greco paints *Coronation of a Saint or a King*.

1570 English mathematician Leonard Digges develops the theodolite.

1575 Spanish writer Cervantes, who had been maimed at the Battle of Lepanto in 1571, is captured by Algerian pirates and held for ransom until 1580.

1560~1612

All the King's Men...

Theatre companies and thespian rivalry

In the 16th century, it was important for any man wanting work to have a master who would employ and vouch for him, for to be 'master-less' meant poverty, homelessness and imprisonment. Actors were subject to this law too. Although out of town troupes of actors had travelled the length and breadth of the land for years, in London it was essential to belong to a company, sponsored by an aristocrat, the Church or the Monarchy.

A watercolour impression of the Globe theatre.

We don't know who Shakespeare worked for when he arrived in London. Some of his early plays were acted by the Earl of Pembroke's Men and the Earl of Sussex's Men, which could suggest that he was with them, but equally it could be that he sold them the plays in a straight deal. But after the plague passed in 1594 (killing some 5 per cent of London's population) and the theatres re-opened, he joined the Lord Chamberlain's Men as actor-playwright, and remained with them until his retirement in 1612. It was the Lord Chamberlain's Men that Shakespeare took to the new Globe, in which he was a shareholder, in 1597, an action which launched the most productive ten years for any theatre company in English history.

The Lord Chamberlain's Men gave Shakespeare the level of stability he needed to write, perform and thus perfect his work. He acted with this company, taking the lead in a play by Jonson (1598) and appearing in most of the performances until around 1604. He also wrote the equivalent of two plays a year, adding them to a repertoire that would have been changed every two days, sometimes daily. Actors then rehearsed one play in the mornings (for a few days) and performed

GROUNDLINGS' GOSSIP

The Lord Chamberlain's Men took out a lease on the Blackfriars indoor theatre, but could not perform there until 1608 (by which time they were the King's Men). Blackfriars allowed them to experiment with such things as artificial light, music and stage effects. They could also charge more – for the privilege of not getting rained on.

1590 Venice's Rialto Bridge is completed, joining the island of Rialto, financial centre of the city, with the island of San Marco.

1603 London has an epidemic of the Black Death that kills at least 33,000 people.

1611 James I's Authorized Version of the Bible is published.

another in the afternoons, while keeping several more in their head at any one time. *Philip HENSLOWE* (d. 1616), owner of the Rose and the Fortune theatres, kept a diary of his business activities in which he records for one month in 1592 that *Henry VI* was performed five times in rotation, along with thirteen other plays.

The Lord Admiral's Men, led by *Edward ALLEYNE* (1566–1626) and based at Philip Henslowe's Fortune theatre near Cripplegate, was a rival company to Shakespeare's, though not,

DRAMATIS PERSONAE

A performance given in 1597 by the Earl of Pembroke's Men of a (now lost) play The Isle of Dogs, by Ben Jonson and Thomas Nashe, apparently contained 'lewd matters', for the delectation of a 'confluence of bad people'. This upset the Privy Council and officers of the Guildhall so much that they called for the theatres to be 'plucked downe'.

The layout of an indoor theatre.

Edward Alleyne demonstrating the classical acting pose for indigestion.

apparently, as well regarded. In 1596 the Lord Chamberlain's Men were invited to give all of the royal command performances for the Christmas season. In 1603, when James I took the throne, they were renamed the King's Men – an honour indeed – while Alleyne's troupe had to make do with being Prince Henry's Men.

Chilly Willy

Generally the companies performed in their London theatres during the winter season, starting at two in the afternoon (after lunch and before the light faded). This meant that actors and audiences would have been out in the winter frost, but it was obviously well worth putting up with the cold. Those who could afford a penny or twopence more could enjoy the shelter of the galleries, while a seat in a private room adjoining the stage was a shilling. The players would tour during summer, to escape the plague and to follow the wealthy, who migrated to the country.

1550 Nicholas Udall writes *Ralph Roister Doister*, the first English comedy.

1581 Italian architect Andrea Palladio dies in Venice, but his books will spread his influence throughout the world.

1590 The archbishop of York accuses English vicar Edward Shawcross of being an 'instructor of young folkes how to comyt the syn of adultrie or fornication and not to beget or bring forth children'.

1550~1625

'The Play's the Thing...'
Shakespeare builds from Roman ruins

Banquo has not been invited for dinner. Some ghosts need to learn some manners.

Elizabethan drama brought together two great dramatic traditions: the classical and the medieval. And the best playwrights, such as Shakespeare, were able to extract the best elements from both and blend them together into a 'new' form.

The classical five-act tragedy format had come from Roman writers such as SENECA (?4 BC–AD 65) and TERENCE (?190–159 BC). ARISTOTLE THE GREEK (384–322 BC) had created the model of a 'complete action' in drama – a beginning, middle and end. An excellent example of Aristotelian action is *Macbeth*, in which Shakespeare created Roman-inspired characters such as the ghost and the messenger, and, best of all, made thrilling use of the soliloquy. Roman drama was also great on comic stock characters such

Mezzetino, one of the stock characters from the *commedia dell'arte*.

DRAMATIS PERSONAE

The visiting Italian theatre groups of the commedia dell'arte *made an impact on London writers*. The Taming of the Shrew *draws upon Italian comedic influences in its* characters, the Bianca subplot and the idea of 'taming' a shrewish wife. But Will added love and, as Edward Quinn said, 'between the guffaw and the smirk, he discovered the smile' (surely he means the 'guffirk'?).

1617 Hired transport is now available in major cities including hackney cabs in London and horse-drawn taxi cabs in Paris.

1620 Edmund Gunter, professor of astronomy at Oxford University, develops the first calculator.

1621 King James issues the 'Book of Sports', permitting a variety of popular sports to be played, and upsets the Puritans.

Dumbing down

'Dumb shows' (part of a play performed in silent pantomime) first appeared in 1561 in *Gorboduc*. Although derived from early comedy, the dumb show could add a powerful dimension to an Elizabethan drama – as in the famous play-within-a-play in *Hamlet*, a pantomimic re-enactment of the murder of Hamlet's father. These days, of course, the phrase is best used to describe your average West End or Broadway hit.

as the bragging soldier, the clever servant or the overwrought father with a teenage daughter (some things never change).

On the private stages, in the schools and the court, the classical forms remained largely unchanged. In the public theatres, however, they were interwoven with more robust forms of medieval theatre, which contributed some excellent dramatic conventions (elements of performance that breathe life into what is otherwise just a piece of writing), such as stock figures, a sense of 'order' in life and a love of allegory and metaphor. But when Elizabeth I died in 1603, so did optimism. The accession of snobby James I ushered in a darker world, reflected in the plays of some of the gloomiest writers, *John WEBSTER*

The Duchess of Malfi discussing a new look with her plastic surgeon.

(?1580–1625) – *The White Devil* (1611) and *The Duchess of Malfi* (1613) – *John MARSTON* (?1576–1634) and *Cyril TOURNEUR* (?1575–1626). Shakespeare's works became more thoughtful, with *Hamlet*, *Macbeth*, *Lear* and *Othello*.

What the Elizabethan dramatists achieved was the bringing together of the classical elements of drama, but in English. Latin had been the only language previously considered capable of delivering any degree of dignity (and, conveniently, it was only understood by the priests and the ruling classes). It was Shakespeare, more than any other, who developed this new drama, in plays that could be clearly understood by his illiterate, if sophisticated, audience.

> ### GROUNDLINGS' GOSSIP
>
> It has been said that one reason why a 2–3 hour show was so popular with Elizabethan audiences was because, compared to all the time they spent sitting through sermons in church, a lengthy drama was no problem. If this is true, then they must also have been great dozing-offers, daydreamers and roof-beam counters.

1553 Lady Jane Grey rules England for nine days until the accession of Mary Tudor.

1590 The game of tennis, originally played against a wall, is developed into a sport for two people with a net between them.

1563 Witchcraft becomes a capital offence in Britain.

1550~1630

Bear-baiting to Blackfriars

Disgraceful actors and disgusting crowds

About one in eight Elizabethan Londoners regularly went to watch theatre performances. The community as a whole was used to live entertainments in their religious festivals, as well as bear-baiting, cock-fighting, prize-fighting and other delights, but theatre was the popular medium. Poetry and prose only reached a limited literate circle.

DRAMATIS PERSONAE

The upper classes were no better behaved. Thomas Dekker (?1572–?1632), in his book The Gull's Hornbook *(1609), describes how 'gallants', having paid sixpence for a stool on the stage, would 'mew at passionate speeches and blare at merry... whistle at the songs and smoke and spit'. The groundlings hated this but if ever one of them cried 'Away with the fool!', warns Dekker, it became 'madness to tarry'!*

The Swan theatre, Southwark, in 1596, by J. de Witt.

Plans for public theatres, such as the Curtain (1576), the Rose (1587), the Swan (1595) and the Globe (1598), show they were adaptable for other 'sports'. The roofless buildings had a 1 metre- (3 ft-) high stage projecting from one wall to the centre of the yard, around which stood the audience. There were galleries for wealthier spectators, and one above the stage for scenes such as Juliet in her bower, a curtained area backstage for 'discoveries' of bodies etc., two side doors for exits and entrances, and the odd trapdoor.

This was *imaginative* theatre at its best, geared to focus on things of true significance – the actor, the action and the audience.

Elizabeth I watching a performance of *The Merry Wives of Windsor*.

1581 The first dramatic ballet, *Ballet Comique de la Reyne* by Italian composer Baltasarini, is staged in Paris.

1618 The 'Defenestration of Prague' by Bohemian Protestants takes place and is a prelude to the Thirty Years' War.

1628 English doctor William Harvey publishes 'On the Motion of the Heart and Blood', describing the circulation of the blood.

The historic first night's performance at the new Globe theatre, London.

Historians often accuse 'groundlings' (so named because they could only afford the open centre ground space) of being no more than a rabble. But even if there were unruly elements, I cannot believe their intention was to interrupt a good story. After all, they had parted with a hard-earned penny – if they were unruly, it would probably have been the weaknesses of the show (or fellow spectators) they resented. Today, between the commercially driven, overpriced and often facile megashows and that tedious *cul de sac* of post-modern, formalist performance art made by and for arty aesthetes, we could do with a bit of unruliness. Ah, me… what a sad day it was when we stopped throwing rotten vegetables at bad actors during bad plays!

GROUNDLINGS' GOSSIP

Elizabethan theatres were the singles bars of their day. Gosson, in his *School of Abuse* (1579), describes the male groundlings' 'heaving and shoving... itching and shouldering' to sit by women. The men went on with much 'toying, smiling and winking', trying to chat them up.

The private indoor theatres that staged Shakespeare's plays, such as Blackfriars, allowed some experimentation with lighting (lots of candles = midday, few candles and torches = night-time). But it was still dialogue or costume that enforced the main distinction between day and night. In other private 'theatres', in halls, courts and colleges with an 'acting' area, 'interludes' (short, mainly comic, after-dinner plays) were performed, as well as masques and pageants.

Hidden scenes

Interestingly, the notion of 'private' entertainment was quite properly regarded by the Elizabethan man in the street with some suspicion. It wasn't seen as an elite activity from which undesirables were *excluded*, which corresponds with the modern interpretation, but rather as a clandestine gathering of egomaniacs who wished to *conceal* some wickedness! Almost as if they'd known about corporate senior management conferences or cabinet meetings.

1616 England's James I begins selling peerages in an attempt to replenish the depleted royal treasury.

1616 Ben Jonson's publication *Poems* includes 'Drink to me only with thine eyes ...'.

1616 The Vatican orders Galileo Galilei to stop defending Copernican 'heresy' and has him arrested.

1616

Will and Testament
Famous last words? Well, yes, actually...

Shakespeare's monument at Stratford-upon-Avon.

No one knows what Shakespeare died of. Fifty years after his death, a rumour sprang up, based on a diary entry of a Stratford vicar, that Shakespeare, Ben Jonson and others had a 'merry meeting' and 'drank too hard'. But whatever it was, on 23 April 1616, he finally shuffled off this mortal coil at the age of 52.

He had retired to Stratford some time after writing *The Tempest* in 1611. At home his days were spent, according to Rowe, 'in Ease, retirement, and the Conversation of his Friends'. He owned land and property and was very famous in Stratford even then. Perhaps the most interesting things about his death are the epitaph he composed for his tombstone, and his Last Will. The epitaph warns:

'Good Frend For Jesus Sake Forbeare
To Digg the Dust Enclosased Heare
Bleste be Ye Man That Spares Thes Stones
And Cursed Be He That Moves My Bones'

Shakespeare bequeathed most of his estate to his daughter Susanna and her husband, John Hall. But it is the exceptions and changes to the will that have caused comment. He made the first version of his will in January, but on 25 March, when he was already frail, he recalled the solicitor,

1616 Japanese samurai Mitsui Sokubei Takatoshi opens a sake and soy sauce establishment and discovers that patrons will pawn their valuables for a drink of sake.

1616 Antwerp's Notre Dame Cathedral is completed after 264 years of construction.

1616 Dutch astronomer-mathematician Willebrord Snellius discovers the law of light refraction.

Lineage

Like all men of that time, Shakespeare hoped for a male heir to pass on what he had earned from a lifetime of art, wit and business acumen. This may be why he left Susanna so much of his estate. He had no surviving son, but his will indicates his bequest to her was to be passed on to 'the first son of her body lawfully issuing'. The will makes no mention of what he wished to happen to his literary output, probably because the whole area of copyright was so unclear that it did not seem worthwhile.

What Shakespeare found at the bottom of his garden! (Arthur Rackham's *Tempest*).

Francis Collins of Warwick, to make changes to the provision for his other daughter, Judith. In February she had married Thomas Quiney, whom Shakespeare did not like, and seemingly with good reason *(see page 19)*. Shakespeare left her £100 plus another £150 if she lived three years more, but he forbade Quiney any claim to the money unless he 'settled on her lands, £150'.

Then there was the 'second best bed' he left to his wife, Anne Hathaway. This was probably the bed they slept in, the best being kept for distinguished visitors. Was this sarcasm, or some kind of private joke, or was it a genuine gift? And why didn't she claim the third of all his goods and property she was entitled to in law as his wife? We'll never know.

In the 1623 Folio, Jonson wrote the following verse in his long and glowing eulogy:
'*Soule of the Age!*
The applause! Delight! The wonder of our Stage!
My Shakespeare, rise.......
Thou art a Moniment, without a tombe'
And art still alive, while thy Booke doth live,
And we have wits to read, and praise to give.'

DRAMATIS PERSONAE

His last surviving sister, Joan Hart, received the use during her lifetime of the Henley Street house where she was living, as well as £30. Each of her sons received £5. Richard Burbage, John Hemings and Henry Condell received 28 shillings and sixpence each to 'buy them ringes' (for memorial purposes). Condell and Hemings would commemorate him in a much more permanent and meaningful way with the First Folio.

1592 The Edinburgh Parliament agrees to the Presbyterian system of church government.

1597 The first crop of domestically grown tomatoes is produced and eaten in England.

1599 In Naples, Tommas Campanello is imprisoned for attempting to lead a revolution and writes *City of the Sun* – a fantasy of an ideal city, ruled by priests through scientific magic.

1592~1612

All That Glitters...

Shakespeare in the city

Was there no end to the Great Man's talents? Not content with being one of the best writers of his generation, he was also smart enough to capitalize on that success and become theatre co-owner, property owner, country gentleman and landowner. And all this in a time when theatre, to say the least,

DRAMATIS PERSONAE

New House was built by Sir Hugh Clopton, who built the Guild Chapel for residents of Stratford and also the bridge over the River Avon carrying the southbound road. Little did young Willy realize, when he crossed that bridge to fame and fortune in London, that he would one day return to buy the house of its builder! By the way, 'Avon' is an old Celtic word for 'river', so it is in fact the River River.

was a most precarious occupation: if it wasn't the Puritans, Mayor and Corporation trying to spoil the fun, there was always bubonic plague.

Shakespeare's financial success was due to a mixture of artistic brilliance and a few lucky breaks. Before his time drama wasn't considered a serious vehicle for 'high' writing; that remained the privilege of poetry and prose. But as Shakespeare well knew, the popular stage was where his talent would flourish. He breathed life into old stories for a appreciative audience. This horrified 'serious'

Cooking the books

Publishing and printing were on the increase, too. In 1600 there were about 100 publishers, of whom 19 were also printers. *Titus Andronicus* was Shakespeare's first play to see print, and when he retired in 1612 about half of his plays had been published – and over half of those actually bore his name.

1600 France's Henri IV marries his niece Marie de' Medici in October and gains control of Tuscany.

1608 John Dee, Queen Elizabeth I's astrologer, dies in extreme poverty.

1610 *The Roaring Girl*, or *Moll Cutpurse*, by Thomas Dekker and Thomas Middleton, is performed at London's Fortune theatre, by the Prince's Men.

Shakespeare directs a private showing of *Macbeth* for Elizabeth I.

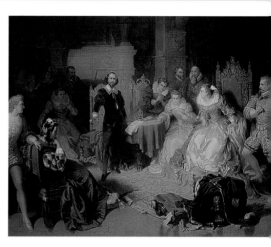

poets but the commercial gains were huge: companies of actors paid £5 or £6 per play (about six months' wages to a carpenter, or eight months of 'feather bed' lodgings).

In 1598, he bought into the newly built Globe as a 'housekeeper' with a one-tenth share, along with Richard and Cuthbert Burbage, Will Kempe, John Heminges, Augustine Phillips, Tom Pope and others. Thus he was able to stage his plays, get paid to act in them and finally take a share of the box-office! In those days a new play went on every few days, was held in a repertory of nine or ten plays and rotated over several weeks. So even though he didn't get royalties, he could generate wealth from volume and repeat orders.

He was thus able to restore his family's lost fortunes, and in 1597 he bought Stratford's biggest house, New Place. He also invested in grain, land rents (or 'tithes') and, in 1601, he bought 100 acres of arable land in Old Stratford. By the time he left London in 1612 to move back to Stratford he was already one of its leading citizens. Later he bought property in Blackfriars. Overall it has been estimated Shakespeare earned between £180 and £200 p.a. which, given that a schoolmaster's salary was between £5 and £20 p.a., is not bad for a thesp!

The south-east prospect of Stratford-upon-Avon, circa 1746.

1450 English longbowmen are blown away by French cannons at the Battle of Formigny.

1463 The importation of playing cards is banned in Britain, to encourage local producers.

1507 Martin Waldseemuller introduces the concept of the 'New World' with his map depicting South America and Asia as separate from each other for the first time.

1450~1650

Master of Revels: Tolerant of Few
And no sex, either!

The Elizabethan winter brought the 'Season of Revels': weeks of festivities ranging from the common, popular knees-ups to court processions. It was a custom from at least the 14th century for a short period of 'misrule' to be tolerated by the ruling class each year as a sort of escape valve for popular dissension.

People in towns and villages were encouraged to contravene, albeit mildly, the normal conventions of behaviour – to act the fool and mock authority. A 'Lord of Misrule', or 'Christmas Lord', was elected locally to 'preside' over the occasion and direct the bad behaviour; and who best to provide that but students and apprentices? At Oxford and Cambridge students would make speeches insulting the Vice Chancellor and staff (Gosh! The cads!), whereas in London apprentices often rioted, attacking brothels, inns and theatres especially (I can think of *much* better targets). In 1617 they burnt down the Cockpit theatre.

Among the aristocracy, seasonal entertainments were much *nicer*. The Season of Revels began on 17 November (the anniversary of Elizabeth's coronation), with music, dancing, masques and theatrical productions (sometimes Shakespeare's plays) in court. The job of

The Lord of Misrule directs the revellers and frolics with his chums.

Schools for fools
Schoolchildren had some respite from their Latin classes by electing a Boy Bishop, from 6 December to the Feast of Holy Innocents on 28 December. This tradition was not unlike the Feast of Fools held on the Continent, during which children would make fun of the Church and go from house to house asking for money.

1534 King Henry VIII breaks away from the Catholic Church and declares himself head of the English Church in order to divorce his wife Catherine of Aragon and marry Anne Boleyn.

1547 Venetian artist Tintoretto paints *The Last Supper.*

1648 The Treaty of Westphalia ends the Thirty Years' War in Germany.

organizing these festivities was given to a 'Master of Revels', who, unlike the 'Lord of Misrule', was not at all tolerant of bad behaviour, or seditious material in plays. The Master of Revels was responsible for choosing plays and actors, and any playwright wanting to include a bit of controversial material, as Shakespeare often did, had to be *very* careful if he wanted to keep his head.

Under Elizabeth the Revels office was frankly one of censorship. From 1579 to 1603, the post was occupied by one Edmund Tilney, a man who took his job very seriously indeed, and any company putting on a play not approved by 'his office' was punished. All scripts were submitted to him for approval – and the company had to pay for the privilege. If he demanded cuts he would refuse to allow a performance until he got them. He was particularly vigilant about passages attacking religion or politics, and also satire (which only leaves sex… and, you've

GROUNDLINGS' GOSSIP

Shakespeare was particularly adroit at avoiding Tilney's displeasure. His history plays, for example, are thinly disguised analyses of contemporary situations, but Tilney allowed them. His tragedies also cover some pretty interesting political issues, but again, they got performed. In any case, censorship can never totally succeed in live performance – there is so much an actor can do with words, intonation, looks, glances, gesture and silence that cannot be struck out of a script.

guessed it, he didn't like that either). The abdication scene in *Richard II*, for example, doesn't appear in any of the editions of the play we know were available during Elizabeth's reign. It is more than possible that Hawkeye Tilney had the offending words removed.

Fiona Shaw as Richard III showing us who wears the trousers.

DRAMATIS PERSONAE

Censorship always has its spies. Ben Jonson, in Bartholomew Fair *(1614), sneers at the 'politic picklock of the scene' – that is, someone who deliberately 'interprets' a performance in such a way that he can* report it to the Master of Revels. His bitterness was personal. In 1605 he co-wrote Eastward Ho!, *which mocked the Scots (well, they are funny), but he was accused of ridiculing King James and was imprisoned.*

1593 London's theatres close for a year because of the plague.

1594 In Florida, Father Balthasar Lopez holds a mass baptism of 80 Indians.

1597 Spanish lyric poet Fernando de Herrera dies in Seville. He is best known for his *canciones* describing the 1571 Battle of Lepanto.

1590~1616

We Only Laugh When it Hurts!

Punishment, prisoners and perky Portia the Pardoner

The Elizabethans were very good at punishment. None other than Sir Walter Raleigh was told in 1603 he was to be 'hanged and cut down alive… [his] body opened… privy members cut off and thrown into the fire… and heart and bowels plucked out'. After that he was to be beheaded and his body quartered. Only two years earlier he had laughed as he watched his old rival the Earl of Essex beheaded for treason. As it turned out Raleigh was lucky; all he had to endure in the end was 13 years in the Tower!

Justice was, as always, a serious business but unlike today (at least in civilized places) a large part of it was vengeance. But mercy was a quality not forgotten and Shakespeare's plays demonstrate the

> ### GROUNDLINGS' GOSSIP
>
> It may surprise you to learn that London's Bridewell prison was intended to provide economic rehabilitation and improvement! The hard labour criminals were forced to do was for their own good, so that they might not 'like to grow to be idle rogues'. Heaven forbid!

The final scene in *Hamlet*, and the sight is dismal. No pardon likely here.

fascination society had for pardon and amnesty as well as revenge. When King James travelled to his new throne in 1603 he pardoned all those held in Berwick prison except those who had been found guilty of 'treason, murder and Papistry'. He even paid the debts of debtors.

Shakespeare's comedies, in particular, explore the tensions between pardon and vengeance. His tragedies might have shown violence in the pursuit of justice, with bodies placed 'high on a stage' (*Hamlet*), but his comedies reveal a fascination with

1610 Monteverdi publishes his *Vespers* in Venice.

1613 The Romanov dynasty begins in Russia and will last until 1917.

1614 Venice's prisons and their connecting Bridge of Sighs are completed after 41 years of work to enlarge the state prison in the Doge's Palace.

The RSC consider the evidence in their 1994 staging of *Measure for Measure*.

the power to pardon. The same year as Raleigh's trial, *Measure for Measure* was performed at court. In it the Duke decides against punishment, for 'having bound up the threatening twigs of birch, / only to stick it in their children's sight / For terror, not to use'. Better to threaten than to hit, which is a step in the right direction. But the play considers the other view: Angelo, who is *really* into 'beheading and hanging', looks 'to find good cause to whip them all', because 'we must not make a scarecrow of the law'.

Shakespeare gave us perhaps the most famous argument for mercy and pardon in the *The Merchant of*

Never mind the mercy, feel the quality. Ellen Terry as Portia.

Venice. Portia declares that 'The quality of mercy is not strain'd' in pleading that power loses nothing by granting pardon. In contrast, mercy 'is above this sceptred sway, It is enthroned in the heart'. And, as she points out to Shylock, mercy is 'twice blest', as it benefits 'him that gives' as much as 'him that takes'. Smart girl, that young Portia!

Transportation troubles

Within six months of his coronation, as an alternative to pardon and re-absorption into English society, James I hit on the brilliant idea of sending 'incorrigible and dangerous rogues' to the 'New found Lands' across the Atlantic. In doing this he started a veritable trend for exporting those who would normally have been hanged. If he could have seen ahead to fast food and theme parks, he might have thought it prudent just to buy more rope.

1567 Mary, Queen of Scots, abdicates in favour of her son James VI.

1612 Musician Orlando Gibbons publishes his 'First set of madrigals and motets of 5 parts, apt for viols and voices'.

1617 Pocahontas, or Lady Rebecca Rolfe, dies during a visit to England.

1550~1950

Bottom is as Bottom does
What's in a name? Pretty well everything

Elizabethan writers had fun when it came to naming their dramatic characters. Ben Jonson had Volpone (the Fox), in the play of the same name, and the hypocritical Puritan character Busy, who was a 'Zeal of the Land', the servant Wasp and the young ingenue, Grace Wellborn, in his Bartholomew Fair. *Shakespeare, too, enjoyed this game, with Bottom, Starveling, Quince and Snout named for their physical attributes or trades in* A Midsummer Night's Dream.

John Ruskin attempted to describe the etymology of Shakespeare's character names in his *Munera Pulveris*. But he went a bit quiet on the subject after Matthew Arnold virtually accused him of making the meanings up. James Joyce, always one for a merry quip, made a *grand* joke in *Ulysses* about Mr and Mrs Shakespeare's names. His protagonist, Stephen Dedalus, says 'If others have their will, Ann hath a way' (....okay, please yourselves).

Some of Shakespeare's names are sound

Justice Shallow scrambling over a stile in *The Merry Wives of Windsor.*

1693 White's chocolate house opens in St James's Street in London.

1748 William Cullen demonstrates the first known artificial refrigeration at Glasgow University.

1925 'The Charleston' is introduced to Paris by 'Bricktop', a red-headed American from Harlem who has become hostess at a Place Pigalle nightclub.

Witty Willy

Shakespeare had fun with his own name, too. In Sonnet 135, he punned on the saying 'A woman will have her will' when he writes, 'Whoever hath her wish, thou hast thy Will, / And Will to boot, and Will in overplus... think all but one, and me in that one Will'. Again, in Sonnet 143, he begins, 'So will I pray that thou mayst have thy Will'.

Malvolio in the RSC's 1991 production of *Twelfth Night*.

'games'. Richard II's executioner is Sir Pierce (ouch!), whereas his equivalent in *Richard III* is Brakenbury (break and bury – good one, eh?). Justice Shallow is named for his brains in *The Merry Wives of Windsor*, and because Macbeth has succumbed to the temptation of evil, he has a servant called Seyton (Satan – I know, you didn't need telling). Shakespeare also played with alliteration: the gaggle of women in *Coriolanus* is Valeria, Virgilia and Volumnia; and there's Hippolyta, Hermia and Helena in *A Midsummer Night's Dream*. In *King Lear*, Cordelia's name comes from the Greek for 'revealed heart'. Goneril seems to suggest gonorrhoea, and Regan sounds a bit like raven, a bird that pecks eyes out. Sometimes he had a bit of a go at someone such as the French (always a popular English sport). In *Henry VI, Part One* he refers to Joan of Arc as 'Joan de Pucelle'. His English hero, Talbot, says '*Pucelle or puzzel, Dolphin or dogfish, / Your hearts I'll stamp out with my horse's heels*'. Naughty, for though 'pucelle' means 'maid' or 'virgin' in medieval French, 'puzzel' means whore in Elizabethan English.

Blind Gloucester's moment of enlightenment on the cliffs of Dover.

DRAMATIS PERSONAE

Twelfth Night *is a good source of entertaining name-play. Orsino was an actual Duke visiting London when the play was written. Olivia sounds like 'I love you' (and Orsino did – at first anyway), but so what? Viola is almost an anagram of Olivia; Toby Belch does just that; and Malvolio, as his name suggests, is the malevolent opposite of Benvolio (*A Midsummer Night's Dream*).

1599 'It is unseasonable and unwholesome in all months that have not an R in their names to eat an oyster,' writes London author Richard Buttes in his book *Dyet's Dry Dinner.*

1600 Annibale Caracci puts the finishing touches to his painting *Flight into Egypt;* by 1604 he is suffering from depression and is no longer able to paint.

1600 English physicist William Gilbert completes his pioneering work 'De Magnete, Magneticisque Corporibus', introducing the terms electric attraction, electric force and magnetic pole.

1599~1601

Danish to Go

A prince gets even and a ghost gets laid

Hamlet (1599–1601) is probably Shakespeare's most famous play, and the 'To be, or not to be' speech, articulating Hamlet's wretched indecisiveness, the most quoted lines from any text. It has also been translated into just about every known language on earth. But why is this? Perhaps it's because most people who see or hear the play like to feel there's a bit of Hamlet in themselves.

Home Sweet Home! Elsinore Castle on a fine day.

Some academics have claimed that Hamlet probably reflects more of Shakespeare's own soul than any other character he created. Not his outward self – Hamlet talks where Shakespeare listened; Hamlet was a prince, Shakespeare a glover's son; Hamlet is indecisive, Shakespeare seems to have been prudent and forthright in the conduct of his affairs.

But both men are reflective, highly intelligent and concerned with moral choices. As Clive James has said, 'Hamlet is what would happen if a great poet grew up to be a prince'.

Hamlet is taken from an ancient Scandinavian story (*Ur-Hamlet*) where Prince Hamlet learns from his father's ghost that his uncle, Claudius, murdered him and married Hamlet's mother, Gertrude. The ghost asks Hamlet to avenge him, without harming Gertie. Hamlet feigns madness to deceive Claudius (and uses hapless visiting actors to present a 'mousetrap' play). He gets sent to England, where no one notices madness. Claudius' counsellor, Polonius, while eavesdropping on Hamlet, gets killed, so Claudius takes out a contract on

DRAMATIS PERSONAE

Hamlet is alone on stage more than any other character in the Shakespearean canon. His is the longest role in Shakespeare's plays and contains more soliloquies than any

other. And since these soliloquies are far more introspective than any others, this has given academics cause for endless theorizing as to why he does what he does (or doesn't do, to be precise).

1600 Tobacco sells in London for its weight in silver shillings and becomes extremely popular among the dandies.

1601 Two fleets arrive from Spain to help the Irish in their rebellion against English rule.

1601 Following the Poor Relief Act in England, a further law is introduced allowing the whipping of vagrants and beggars.

Hamlet. Hamlet's girl, Ophelia (Polonius' daughter), goes mad with stress – understandable, some of the audience are heading this way by now – and is found drowned, so her distraught brother Laertes comes to get revenge. By the end Hamlet, Laertes, Gertrude and Claudius all die too. To put it briefly, it's 'Whinge, whinge... Look at me, I'm gaga! Oops, I killed your dad… they're all out to get me…I'm dead!'

Some actors think that landing the part of Hamlet is the ultimate thespian achievement. But they're often the sort who believe great roles make great actors rather than the other way round. It's all that *thinking* he does, you see – it gives a chap Great Scope for Big Acting With Many Pensive And Anguished Looks. Highly satisfying – or so I'm told.

Ophelia considering a trip down the river.

> ### GROUNDLINGS' GOSSIP
>
> Hundreds of works have titles based on *Hamlet* quotations, e.g. Henry J. Jordan's *'To Be or Not To Be, Happiness or Misery? That Is the Question.' Being Four Lectures on the Functions and Disorders of the Nervous System and the Reproductive Organs.* And Monk Ferris' *Hamlet, Cha-Cha-Cha: A Totally Looney Musical Comedy.*

'Alas, poor Yorick! He should have had my agent!' Olivier as Hamlet.

Evacuating the soul

Hamlet is a tragedy, a form that began with the Greeks and was about social and personal anxiety (a constant state for me these days). Aristotle wrote much on tragedy, but sometimes not very clearly. Centrally, there's 'catharsis', apparently meaning a 'purging' or 'purification' for the audience through their feelings of pity and fear for the protagonist. So tragedy is a sort of laxative for the soul.

1606 The Russian pretender, an imposter claiming to be the 'son of Demetrius', is driven from the throne and is murdered by Boris Godunov.

1606 *The Whore of Babylon* by Thomas Dekker is performed by Prince Henry's Men.

1606 Sailors aboard the Dutch ship *Duyjken* become the first Europeans to sight Australia.

1606
Scots on the Rocks
The man who would be king

Hubble, bubble, toil and trouble

This is the play that dare not speak its name – at least not inside a theatre. I'll give you a clue. It starts with 'M', one word, two syllables. First syllable: you wear it in the rain. Actors daren't *mention it: they're such a superstitious lot, they have to refer to it as 'the Scottish play'. Yes, it's* Macb*th. *It's a short play compared to* Hamlet – *one explanation for this is that it was performed (even written) for King James, who had a notoriously low boredom threshold. The plot was largely derived from a story in Holinshed's* Chronicles, *like so many others.*

> ### GROUNDLINGS' GOSSIP
>
> Some actors will never quote from *Macbeth* before or after a performance. Some really believe that the witches' spells can come true and summon up demons (usually these people are in contact with the mother ship). If anyone does mention the 'M' word, they must leave the theatre, turn around three times, spit, and ask permission to re-enter (by which time someone's locked the door).

Macbeth instructing the murderers, by George Cattermole (mid-1880s).

This particular yarn concerns itself with Macbeth, a Scottish 'thane', or lord, of Glamis, who desires to be King of Scotland. He is introduced to us as a war hero, but his fate takes another path when he meets three witches (as one does) who tell him he is destined to become king. Lady Macbeth hears of this and decides to accelerate events by despatching the present king, Duncan. She gets her husband to do it (typical!). Macbeth then frames two hapless grooms and kills them before they can say 'But...but...we were watching TV, Y'r Honour...'. Duncan's sons, Malcolm and Donalbain, run off, thinking they're next. Macbeth is crowned king, but mindful of the witches' other prophecy – that the descendants of his friend Banquo will also be kings – he orders the murder of Banquo and his son Fleance (who escapes). Macbeth has a

1606 France's Henri IV says that if he were to live another ten years 'there would not be a peasant so poor in all my realm who would not have a chicken in his pot every Sunday'.

1606 South Pacific islands that will be named the New Hebrides in 1774 are discovered by Portuguese explorer Pedro Fernandes de Queiros.

1606 The Union Jack is adopted as the British flag.

second consultation with the witches, who warn him to fear Macduff (Thane of Fife), but that no man of woman born can harm him and that he is safe until Birnam Wood advances to Dunsinane Hill. Naturally, he relaxes a bit, but nevertheless orders Macduff's family killed. Macduff joins with Malcolm, who has an army in England. By now Lady Macbeth is a few clowns short of a circus, goes mad and dies. Macduff's army returns, hides behind branches cut from Birnam Wood (drat!), meets Macbeth at Dunsinane and they fight. Macduff ('From his mother's womb / Untimely ripped'... double drat!) kills Macbeth and Malcolm becomes king. I need a lie down.

Unusually for Shakespeare there are no subplots in *Macbeth*. The story is about consequences – guilt, the hardening of the soul, becoming inured to evil. As Lady

> **DRAMATIS PERSONAE**
> Superstition apart, the play does appear to have been cursed with bad luck. In the original performance in 1606, it is said that Hal Berridge, the boy actor playing Lady Macbeth, died. It is also rumoured that Shakespeare himself stepped in to play her role, but at 42, portly and bearded, he must have looked more like a pantomime dame!

Lady Macbeth doing a bit of pre-murder lurking in corridors.

Macbeth's doctor tells her, '*Unnatural deeds / Do breed unnatural troubles*' (what the doctor should, in fact, have done is given her Prozac and notified her shrink about her obsessive-compulsive disorders).

Macbeth is one of Shakespeare's most successful works because it uses the language of theatre so well. There are rapidly recurring motifs in the setting, language and action – night-time, darkness, blood, death, madness and the supernatural – which mirror the horrors in the minds of Lord and Lady M. All good clean stuff.

It's the crazy eyes and ever-ready sword that give it away. Roy Marsden as Macbeth.

1597 Akbar the Great orders that Indian peasants pay him one-third of the gross produce their fields are expected to yield.

1597 Amiens is captured by Archduke Albert of Austria and retaken by Henri IV.

1597 The first English mention of tea appears in a translation of *Travels* by Dutch navigator Jan Huygen van Linschooten. Van Linschooten calls the beverage 'chaa'.

1597
And it's 'Hello Mr Nasty!'
(Tricky Dicky'd give anyone the hump)

There's nothing quite lik[e]
a false nose... Laurenc[e]
Olivier as Richard I[II]

Richard III may have been Shakespeare's first dramatic success. Also based on Holinshed's Chronicles, *it tells the story of another nobleman who wants to be king – Richard of Gloucester, this time. But this one intends to be 'subtle, false and treacherous' to achieve his heart's desire, and the fact that he announces this to the audience in the first few minutes of the play fills us with a delicious sense of anticipation. His two elder brothers, George, Duke of Clarence, and King Edward IV, have to be disposed of first, so he murders Clarence, and Edward conveniently falls ill and dies.*

But Edward, blast him, has two sons, Edward junior (heir to the throne) and little Richard, so Gloucester throws them in the Tower (spare the rod, spoil the child, I always say). He then spreads rumours that they are bastards, and gets himself declared king. After he is crowned he decides to bump off the princes in the Tower – and Clarence's children, too, just for good measure. However (and there's always one of them), the Earl of Richmond, exiled in France but also wanting the throne, returns to England and challenges Richard. They meet at Bosworth Field, and Richard gets his comeuppance. Richmond takes the throne, and Hey Presto! here's Henry VII, the first Tudor king, who marries Princess Elizabeth, thus ending the Wars of the Roses between the

> **GROUNDLINGS' GOSSIP**
>
> **I**t's said that more things have gone wrong during performances of *Richard III* than in any other play (though *Macbeth*'s a serious contender). According to William Hogarth, a former chairman of the Richard III Society's American branch, one 19th-century actor came on stage late in his career, began with 'Now is the winter of our discontent... oh, rubbish!', stripped stark naked and went nuts.

1597 Spain's Philip II sends a second armada against England but a storm scatters his ships once again.

1597 A Muscovite decree demands that runaway serfs be seized and returned to their masters.

1597 Iceland's Mount Hekla volcano erupts.

houses of York and Lancaster. Naturally, all England rejoices. This play might not have proved so popular over the years if it hadn't been for the thorough awfulness of Richard's character, which has been relished with glee by actors and audiences alike. He dominates the play, and has ten soliloquies, of which the famous 'Now is the winter of our discontent…', delivered as soon as he walks on stage, immediately reveals what a foul creature he is.

Yet it seems the real Richard wasn't such a nasty piece of work after all. Shakespeare was probably influenced by Tudor

DRAMATIS PERSONAE

There is no evidence for the story that James Tyrell, Master of the Horse to Richard III, smothered the young princes, or that he buried their bodies at the foot of a flight of stairs in the Tower.

However, in 1674, children's bones were discovered within the foundations of a staircase in the Tower. In 1933 they were exhumed and declared to be the bones of the princes.

The Princes in the Tower, by Sir John Everett Millais (1878).

The Colley-peck

Colley Cibber created a condensed version of *Richard III*, which ran less than two hours (and ousted Shakespeare's version from the English stage for 200 years). Cibber added more blood and guts, and a scene showing the murder of the Princes. He also played Richard like 'the distorted heavings of an unjointed caterpillar'. Nothing like a bit of lively entertainment, is there?

If you can't fight, keep your hair on! Kean as Richard III, by T.C. Wageman.

writings about Richard, which toed the party line: Richard was a 'Yorkist', and thus an enemy of the throne. There are now Richard III societies all over the place, presenting lectures dedicated to clearing his name, and revealing the true story of his life. Apparently he was really a stand-up guy – as straight as the next man!

1594 The Italian painter Tintoretto dies in Venice aged 75.

1594 Lisbon closes her spice market to the English and Dutch, so the Dutch East India Company is formed to obtain spices directly from Asia.

1594 English novelist-playwright Thomas Nashe's *The Unfortunate Traveller, or The Life of Jack Wilton* pioneers the adventure novel.

1594~1595

Have You Been at Those Mushrooms Again, Will?
A Midsummer Night's Dream

Probably written for a nobleman's wedding, A Midsummer Night's Dream *has four interwoven plot lines, all of which are mainly Shakespeare's own invention, with a bit of folklore mixed in.*

The unifying thread is the approaching wedding between Theseus, Duke of Athens, and Hippolyta, Queen of the Amazons. A thoroughly love-tangled quartet, Lysander, Demetrius, Hermia and Helena, get very worked up, and there are some rustic comic characters and assorted fairies and woodland sprites. Oh yes, and there's Oberon and Titania, the King and Queen of the fairies. The play is mostly set in the woods outside Athens, partly because of the wedding, but also because in such an environment Shakespeare can create a magical and supernatural world to contrast with the real one of Theseus, Hippolyta and, of course, the audience. The other plots revolve around the lovers defying parental

Bottom making an ass of himself with the fairies (by Arthur Rackham).

All that mooning around
That old silvery moon exerts a big influence over the action in *A Midsummer Night's Dream*. It's mentioned 28 times (the Bardic average is just a quarter of that), thus contributing to the play's evocation of an enchanted world. The lovers must marry under a new moon, 'like to a silver bow, New-bent in heaven'. Ahhh...

authority, Oberon and his servant, Puck, interfering in the affairs of the mortals, and the 'Pyramus and Thisbe' play put on by Bottom and his friends.

But the point about this play is not its story. It is the brilliant evocation, dark at times, of wonder, magic and romance. Shakespeare masterfully couples the resources of his theatre with the realities, fantasies and mythologies of everyday life. The Elizabethan audience's world of May Day festivals, midsummer night enchantments and faith in the powers of nature is here linked to its darker roots through poetry, wisdom and reason in a play ostensibly about love and authority. Puck's comment 'Lord, what fools these mortals be' refers not only to the young lovers, but also to those in the real world who would presume too much. The 'fairy'

1595 The University of Cambridge is divided over the issue of predestination; the Queen intervenes and calls a halt to the discussions.

1595 Basque whaling captain François Sopite Zaburu devises the world's first factory ship with a brick furnace to extract whale oil from blubber on board ship.

1595 English Jesuit poet Robert Southwell is tried for treason (that is, being a Catholic priest), found guilty and hanged at Tyburn.

GROUNDLINGS' GOSSIP

A *Midsummer Night's Dream* doesn't show humankind – or fairykind, come to that – in a good light (but then, not many of Shakespeare's plays do). Oberon humiliates Titania with Bottom, just to get his own way, and Theseus, in winning Hippolyta, resorts to violence: '*I woo'd thee with my sword, / And won thy love doing thee injuries*'. And a whole load can be read into that!

world – where humans may experience fear and humiliation – is a necessary one.

The play also mocks two of the greatest 'evils' that so upset the Puritans, namely the imitation of human speech and actions (which they saw as falsehood), and men dressing up as women (the very thought of which made Puritan men walk funny). Shakespeare was a great poet of the theatre who put trust in the audience's willing suspension of disbelief, a natural attribute of the human imagination. What's hard to believe is that the Puritans had trouble with that.

The little people

The festivities of Midsummer's Eve and Midsummer Day were traditionally occasions when fairies and other sprites made themselves visible to humans – though the quaffing of great amounts of rough cider may have had some bearing on that. They were also popular dates for the Mystery Plays to be performed.

RUPERT
EVERETT

CALISTA
FLOCKHART

KEVIN
KLINE

MICHELLE
PFEIFFER

STANLEY
TUCCI

A WILLIAM
SHAKESPEARE'S

MIDSUMMER
NIGHT'S
DREAM PG

Love makes fools of us all.

'All Star Cast in Woodland Rave.' Michael Hoffman's 1999 film of the *Dream*.

1605 Catherine de Vivonne de Savelli, Marquise de Rambouillet, finding Parisian society too coarse, makes her home a centre for refined and witty conversation and creates the first great Paris 'salon'.

1605 Guy Fawkes' Gunpowder Plot to blow up the Houses of Parliament fails when 36 barrels of gunpowder are discovered in the cellars of the building.

1605 The world's first newspaper begins publication in Antwerp under the direction of local printer Abraham Verkoeven, a notorious drunk.

1605
'Nothing Comes of Nothing'
Goldi-Lear and the three daughters

The original story of King Lear *first appeared in Geoffrey of Monmouth's* Historia Regum Brittaniae *(1137), but Shakespeare got most of his information from the Holinshed* Chronicles, *Edmund Spenser's* The Faerie Queen *and an anonymous play,* The True Chronicle History of King Leir and His Three Daughters *(1590), and the Gloucester subplot from Sir Philip Sydney's* Arcadia. *So now you know.*

The story concerns a doddery old king who divides his lands between his three daughters, Goneril, Regan and Cordelia, according to how well each describes her love for him (not the smartest way to start one's retirement). Goneril and Regan flatter him, whereas Cordelia, the youngest, simply says she loves him as a daughter should. Enraged at her candour and lack of flattery, Lear throws her out and the King of France takes her home with him (hmm). Now Goneril and Regan show him how much they love him by disallowing him his followers and showing him little respect. Enraged, he will not remain with either of them, leaves to wander the 'blasted heath' and takes leave of his senses. But the (truly) loyal Earl of Kent, though

previously banished by Lear for sticking up for poor Cordelia, disguises himself and takes Lear to Dover to meet the French army, and Cordelia, come to sort out Goneril and Regan. Lear regains his sanity, but is captured. Cordelia is hanged, and Lear dies heartbroken with her in his arms.

I want my mummy!

In *King Lear*, there are no mothers; instead there is a patriarchal environment in which children owe their existence only to their father. And look what happens! Not surprisingly, Freudians and feminists have had a field day with this.

1605 The first railway in Britain is constructed, at Wollaton in Nottinghamshire.

1605 England claims Barbados.

1605 Miguel Cervantes' novel *Don Quixote* is published in Spain, concerning a priest who likes tilting at windmills.

The subplot concerns Edmund, bastard son of the Duke of Gloucester, and his good brother Edgar. Edgar flees from scary Edmund, wanders as a madman, and meets Lear, now united with Edmund's father, who has been blinded and cast out. Gloucester then dies in peace. Goneril and Regan have both turned their affections towards Edmund. Embittered by this rivalry, jealous Goneril poisons Regan and commits suicide. A disguised Edgar kills Edmund who cries 'The wheel is come full circle'. Not many jokes here.

King Lear is Shakespeare's most profound play. It seems as if he is intent upon opening up a chasm in the meaning of existence itself, and revealing nothing but nothingness. The word 'nothing' crops up time and again. All is bleak, anarchic,

Cordelia says the wrong thing to Papa.

Who's playing the fool now?
Ironically, the Fool's role in *King Lear*, which takes much from the traditions of the clown, was to counteract the King's stupidity. The Fool points out that the King is the *real* fool after the love test and division of the Kingdom. After his madness, Lear comes to his senses and the Fool disappears from the action.

> **GROUNDLINGS' GOSSIP**
>
> In Elizabethan times, madness was often thought to be caused by demonic possession. Edgar, disguised as Mad Tom on the heath, talks of ratsbane, a poison widely believed to trigger such insanity. He mentions the devil following him and leading him into the fire. I deduce therefore that ratsbane's what they serve at my local.

Lear holding Cordelia as he realizes what he has done.

senseless – right down to Cordelia's death, which could so easily have been prevented. Some of the basest human instincts are explored and natural laws are subverted, as father turns against child, child turns against father, friend turns to foe, and loyalty and love go unrewarded.

By dividing the kingdom – in effect, decentralizing power – society is seen to be destabilized, especially as it's done without any regard for proper management of the existing economic, political and societal structures. You can see why when Cromwell came along he thought it best to get rid of all this nonsense!

1604 Inigo Jones designs Ben Jonson's production *The Mask of Blackness* for James I.

1604 The Treaty of London is signed, bringing peace between Britain and Spain.

1604 The anonymous pamphlet 'The Triumphant Chariot of Antimony' introduces a new name for stibium, and encourages European physicians to use antimony salts as a homeopathic remedy for fever.

1604

The Moor I See You
(The worse it gets)

Othello: a noble soldier 'perplexed in the extreme'.

Here's another one that's good for a giggle, I don't think. We're back with the fading fortunes of the rich and famous, but this time there are no kingdoms at risk, no rulers toppled, not a usurper in sight. Just an Elizabethan soap opera about a famous general who thinks his wife's having it away with another man, so he kills her. Shakespeare scholar Caroline Spurgeon has defined the prevailing image of the drama as one of 'animals in action, preying upon one another, cruel and suffering … a general sense of pain and unpleasantness is … kept constantly before us'. Like I said before: just another soap opera.

Speed kills

Shakespeare uses time to aid characterization in a very interesting and theatrical way in this play. After the first act, the events take place in less than two days. But the action on stage seems to cover a much longer period. This 'compression' of time forces Othello to act without thought, and to be a slave to his passions. I know just how he feels.

The story begins in Venice where Iago is angry at being passed over for army promotion by his general, Othello the Moor. The promotion went instead to the inexperienced Cassio. Othello secretly marries Desdemona, daughter of Senator Brabantio, against her father's wishes. Military duty takes them to Cyprus, where Iago, bent on revenge, ingratiates himself with Othello and tells

1604 The Hampton Court Conference meets to discuss Church reforms in Britain.

1604 El Greco paints *St Ildefonso*.

1604 In Paris, the Pont Neuf across the Seine is the city's first paved bridge and is lined with houses and shops.

DRAMATIS PERSONAE

The critic Thomas Rymer disliked Shakespeare's language intensely. Fancying himself a man of rational science, he complained that the Bard's words were too fulsome: 'In a Play one should speak like a man of business,' instead of having lines composed of 'this trick of Metaphors, this volubility of Tongue, which makes so great a noise in the world.'

Laurence Fishburne and Kenneth Branagh as Othello and Iago.

him Desdemona is sleeping with Cassio. Othello demands proof, so Iago plants a handkerchief (Othello's gift to Desdemona) in Cassio's room. Othello's discovery of the handkerchief engenders within him doubt and suspicion of such force that he is totally overwhelmed. He becomes so consumed by passion that his murder of Desdemona is the inevitable outcome. At the end, Iago's treachery is revealed, and Othello stabs himself crying that he 'lov'd not wisely, but too well'. Hmm.

The play is about deception and self-deception, lust and hate, insecurity and obsession. It has also been seen as a study of motiveless malignity. 'Honest Iago' spends so much time explaining his actions that it is almost as if he himself is struggling to find a reason for his terrible destructive impulses.

The terrible results of Othello's jealousy and Iago's scheming are shown in this painting by the Italian artist Pompeo Momenti (1819–94).

GROUNDLINGS' GOSSIP

*O*thello is full of animal images, most of which are of insects and other creepy-crawlies. Iago gets to mention plagues of flies, spiders catching flies, monkeys, wild cats and goats. Othello sees his world as full of foul toads, flies and the 'monster ... too hideous to be shown' (no, it's not anything rude – it's all in the mind).

1611 Painter Peter Paul Rubens completes his *Descent from the Cross*.

1611 George Chapman finishes his translation of Homer's *Iliad*.

1611 Potosi in the South American Andes reaches its population peak of 160,000 as the Spanish employ Indian labour to produce tons of silver for shipment back to Spain.

1611

The Island of Doctor Prospero
Enchanted, I'm ashore

Caliban and Ariel doing what comes naturally. (Arthur Rackham)

The Tempest (1611) was Will's last play, at least the last that was entirely his own work. And what a piece of supreme imagination and allegory it is too. Unusually, there are no certain sources for the story, so it looks as if he actually did make this one up! Academics have read all sorts into this play, especially with it being his final offering. He has Prospero deliver his retirement speech:

'Our revels now are ended. These our actors
As I foretold you, were all spirits, and
Are melted into air, into thin air…
…the great globe itself
Yea, all which it inherit, shall dissolve
And, like this unsubstantial pageant faded,
Leave not a rack behind.'

Even the final two lines of the Epilogue: *'As you from crimes would pardon'd be, / Let your indulgence set me free'*, are taken by some as his personal farewell to the stage. The story centres on an enchanted island inhabited by a magician, Prospero, his daughter, Miranda, his slave, the half-monster Caliban and a spirit servant, Ariel. He is there because his brother, Antonio, in cahoots with Alonzo, King of Naples, drove him from his dukedom in Milan some years earlier. The play begins as Antonio, Alonzo, his brother Sebastian, Alonzo's son Ferdinand, the jester Trinculo and the drunken butler Stephano are shipwrecked on his island by a storm at sea – a storm caused by Prospero's magic. Ariel bewitches Ferdinand so that he falls in love with Miranda. Antonio and Sebastian find Alonzo asleep and plan to murder him, but Ariel stops them. Caliban suggests to Trinculo and Stephano that they murder

Elizabethan FX
The Tempest is one of Shakespeare's most *aural* plays. From the outset he puts us 'On a ship at sea: a tempestuous noise of thunder and lightning heard' (Folio stage directions). On the island you should be able to hear the sound of wild beasts, making 'a din to frighten a monster's ear'. And all this would have been done with drums, trumpets and metallic crashes.

1611 Denmark declares war on Sweden after more than 40 years of peace, and hostilities continue until 1613.

1611 Playwright Cyril Tourneur writes *The Atheist's Tragedy, or The Honest Man's Revenge.*

1611 The University of Santo Tomás is founded at Manila in the Philippines.

Prospero to release him from slavery, but Ariel squashes this plan too. Finally Prospero gets everyone before him, forgives them and prepares to return home as Duke of Milan once again. Pretty simple really.

Some scholars have suggested the whole play is an allegory for Shakespeare's life, and that Prospero, in the way that he 'scripts and directs' the action with his magic, represents Shakespeare

William Hamilton's vision of *The Tempest*. Prospero summons Ariel in true Victorian style.

himself. But whatever people dream up, *The Tempest* is a beautiful allegorical story about art and nature, reality and illusion, death and immortality.

It is what Wordsworth called a 'journey of the mind', written for an audience who had no trouble understanding its complexities as a tale of the here and now, yet could also appreciate it as an imaginative and magical parable.

GROUNDLINGS' GOSSIP

Laurens van der Post pointed out that Ariel and Caliban had been on the island for 12 years, then Prospero spent 12 years there. The first 12 years, claimed Van der Post, was the time from when Shakespeare started writing to the crisis that was the 'Hamlet in himself', and another 12 years passed until he wrote *The Tempest,* thus finding 'his own individual island self'. It takes all sorts.

Stephano recommends the house red to Trinculo and Caliban.

1597 The first opera, *La Dafne*, is privately staged at carnival time at the Corsi Palazzo in Florence, with music by Jacopo Peri adopting the recitative musical form used by the ancient Greeks in their tragedies.

1597 Hammocks are authorized by the Admiralty for use on royal naval vessels.

1597 The blackness of Queen Elizabeth's teeth is noted by German traveller Paul Henter, who ascribes it to excessive consumption of sugar – the first time sugar and tooth decay are linked.

1597

Keeping it in the Family
Romeo, Juliet and the course of true love

The Tragedy of Romeo and Juliet *was first published in a quarto edition of 1597. This play, one of the bawdiest, is also one of the most popular of William's works. It has been used as a basis for many love stories, not least of which was* West Side Story, *the musical.*

The Sharks and Jets meet on the street, in the 1961 film, *West Side Story*.

In Verona there are two warring families, the Montagues and the Capulets. Romeo Montague goes to a ball to see Rosaline, the girl with whom he is smitten but who has rejected him, and there meets young Juliet Capulet. They fall in love, and secretly marry. Tybalt Capulet, an angry young man who spotted Romeo gatecrashing the ball, challenges Romeo to fight. He declines, but his charismatic friend

Mercutio accepts on his behalf, and gets himself killed. Romeo, now filled with a fury, kills Tybalt, so the Prince of Verona banishes him. Meanwhile, Juliet's father arranges for her to be married off to Count Paris. Feeling sorry for her, a friar, Laurence, gives her a potion that will simulate death (scrumpy's quite good for

'It'll be better when we get our own place.'

Filthy habits
Arguably the eventual catastrophe was all down to Friar Laurence and his potion. Where did he get these ideas? Well, monks had a history of such things. After the Dissolution of the Monasteries many stories emerged about convent fishponds full of foetal skeletons, and young boys drugged and lured in to be catamites (sex toys) for the monks.

1597 Famous for his lute playing and ballad singing, John Dowland publishes his *First Book of Songs*.

1597 Dutch navigator Willem Barents dies in the Arctic, ending his effort to discover the Northeast Passage.

1597 James VI of Scotland publishes his *Demonologie*, on witchcraft.

that, too), to be taken on the eve of her wedding. Romeo will then come to steal her away while everyone thinks she is dead. But everything goes wrong. Romeo isn't told of the potion. He finds her apparently 'dead', so he poisons himself. Juliet awakes, finds Romeo dead, and kills herself – properly this time, with a big knife. Finally both families come to realize that their silly feuding was the real cause of all this.

Mercutio adds a sparkle to this rather sentimental story with his wit, innuendo and ribaldry. Here's his advice to Romeo (basically, to stop swanning around indulging his ideas of 'courtly love' and to get on with the sex), wherein 'bauble' means penis, as does 'tale', and I can't *bring* myself to say what 'hole', 'depth', or 'hair' represent!

MERCUTIO: *For this drivelling love is like a great natural, that runs lolling up and down to hide his bauble in a hole.*

BENVOLIO: *Stop there, stop there.*

MERCUTIO: *Thou desirest me to stop in my tale against the hair.*

BENVOLIO: *Thou wouldst else have made thy tale large.*

Olivia Hussey mourns over Leonard Whiting in Zeffirelli's 1968 film.

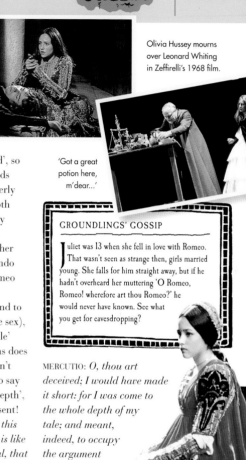

'Got a great potion here, m'dear...'

GROUNDLINGS' GOSSIP

Juliet was 13 when she fell in love with Romeo. That wasn't seen as strange then, girls married young. She falls for him straight away, but if he hadn't overheard her muttering 'O Romeo, Romeo! wherefore art thou Romeo?' he would never have known. See what you get for eavesdropping?

MERCUTIO: *O, thou art deceived; I would have made it short: for I was come to the whole depth of my tale; and meant, indeed, to occupy the argument no longer.*

Juliet wonders if she'd be better off going to college.

Pot pourri

It's been proposed that the phrase 'That which we call a rose by any other name would smell as sweet' is an insult to the rival Rose theatre. The Rose apparently left an area round back to be used as an open-air loo, and performances were just as famous for their stink as for their artistic qualities.

1590 The Black Death reaches Rome and several other Italian cities.

1592 The ruined city of Pompeii is discovered; lava has mummified former occupants in exactly the position they were in when disaster struck.

1594 The sweet potato reaches China 30 years after being introduced by the Spanish into the Philippines.

1590~1608

The Roman Plays
Toga trouble with Titus, Tony, Timon and team

Shakespeare's 'Roman' plays were written over a period of nearly 20 years, and are grouped together as mainly tragic stories of events taking place in ancient Greece or Rome. They are not as popular as his other plays, at least not the later ones.

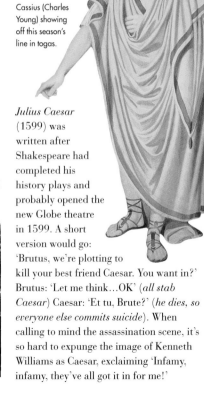

Cassius (Charles Young) showing off this season's line in togas.

Titus Andronicus (1590–94) is a revenge tragedy first produced, according to Philip Henslowe's *Diary*, in 1594. There is no definitive source for the play, but it's influenced by Roman classical structures (and their love of nasty deaths). Titus takes Goth Queen Tamora captive then sacrifices her eldest son, which she doesn't like at all. He then tries to marry off his daughter to someone she doesn't love, so she runs away with someone she does. Her jilted suitor, the Emperor of Rome, marries Tamora and they plot to kill Titus. Nearly everyone dies by the end.

Julius Caesar (1599) was written after Shakespeare had completed his history plays and probably opened the new Globe theatre in 1599. A short version would go: 'Brutus, we're plotting to kill your best friend Caesar. You want in?' Brutus: 'Let me think…OK' (*all stab Caesar*) Caesar: 'Et tu, Brute?' (*he dies, so everyone else commits suicide*). When calling to mind the assassination scene, it's so hard to expunge the image of Kenneth Williams as Caesar, exclaiming 'Infamy, infamy, they've all got it in for me!'

> ### GROUNDLINGS' GOSSIP
>
> The Globe production of *Julius Caesar* was witnessed by a Swiss tourist, Thomas Platter. After the play, he wrote that there came a 'most elegant and curious dance, two men dressed in men's clothes and two in women's'! *Julius Caesar* also contained chiming clocks, feather hats, chimney pots and bound books, all unknown in ancient Rome.

1596 English poet Sir John Harington writes the satirical 'Metamorphosis of Ajax' and is banished from the court as a result.

1600 A law is passed in Central and South American Spanish colonies forbidding whites to enter Indian villages without permission.

1603 Carlo Maderno completes Castel Gondolfo, the pope's summer residence 45 km (28 miles) southeast of Rome.

Antony and Cleopatra (1607) is drawn from Plutarch's *Life of Antony*. It concerns Mark Antony in Egypt and how his love of Cleopatra has reduced him to a life of idle gluttony. When Caesar marches on Egypt, Antony's not sure which side to fight on. Cleopatra sends a false report that she's dead, so he thinks it best to kill himself, but just before he dies he hears she's still alive.

Toby Stevens going scary in the RSC's *Coriolanus*.

There are flaws and loose ends in *Timon of Athens* (1607–1608), so it's generally considered unfinished. It concerns a rich and generous nobleman, Timon, who goes bankrupt, is ignored by his fair-weather friends, finds gold in the woods, gives it to

enemies of Athens but not to his friends. His tomb is found by the seashore, its epitaph expressing his hatred of mankind.

Coriolanus (1608) concerns the rise and fall of a man you really wouldn't want at your birthday party. He is a military hero, an egotist, quick to anger, has no common sense and is dominated by his mother... and even she describes his actions against Rome as 'tearing his country's bowels out', while others describe him as a 'diseased limb and gangrened foot'. He also has no concern for his office or his people and is unfit to rule. Not a popular one, except among MPs.

Play postponed

There are no records of performances of *Timon of Athens*, *Coriolanus* or *Antony and Cleopatra* during Shakespeare's period (nor have they really had much success since, although audiences look more kindly on Ant and Cleo now). In fact it is very unlikely that *Timon of Athens* was ever produced in Jacobean times because of its patchy state.

Such decadence! Ant and Cleo (Alan Rickman and Helen Mirren) live it up.

1591 French mathematician François Viète introduces an algebraic system using alphabetical symbols.

$$x-y=z$$
$$m(2z+y)$$
$$z(m-x)$$

1591 Queen Elizabeth I founds Trinity College, Dublin.

1592 After 294 years of construction, Florence's Palazza Vecchio is completed.

BACK LATER

1590~1597

The Henrys – Men of Many Parts
Henry VI and Henry IV

Rewriting history

Shakespeare's Histories, like the Tragedies and Comedies, are so called because that's how they were grouped in the 1623 First Folio – and also because... well, they're about history. Since then, naturally, scholars have disagreed as to which plays fit in here. Basically, the history play focuses on events and nationality, while tragedy and comedy deal with character first. But as all these things get interwoven in Shakespeare's drama, this is very imprecise.

H enry VI Parts One, Two and Three (1590–92) were written as a trilogy and dealt with the Wars of the Roses. The history they contained was neither objective nor impartial, reflecting Holinshed, their Tudor source. *Part One* begins on the battlefields of France. Henry V gets killed and a young Henry VI takes the throne, while Gloucester acts as caretaker. Cardinal Beaufort, Gloucester's enemy, starts a fight. Somerset, of Lancaster, then fights with Plantagenet, of York. Joan of Arc (portrayed as a sorceress) fights Talbot of England in France. Talbot is killed; Joan gets burned. *Part Two* has Suffolk arrange the marriage of young Henry to Margaret of Anjou. Thus Suffolk and Margaret rule since Henry is a wimp. Suffolk kills Gloucester, gets banished and

> **Garden of England**
> The predominant imagery of the Henry plays is of fruit, flowers and weeds from early growth to final decay brought on by careless and ignorant gardeners. Some metaphors refer to the badges of York and Lancaster while others suggest that a king's death means that the roots of society are going to wither.

'Don't cry, sir. We'll wash it off when we get home.'

1593 Henri IV of France turns Catholic after attending mass at St Denis.

1594 Sculptor Giovanni de Bologna erects equestrian statues of Cosimo I and Ferdinando in Florence.

Falstaff plays at being King in *Henry IV, Part One*. Pity the chair.

killed by pirates. Enter the revolting peasants led by Jack Cade – but Cade gets killed so peasants go home. Meanwhile, back at the castle, Richard of York announces he should be king (as a way of getting out of growing bananas in Virginia), claiming longer royal lineage than Henry's family. (Cue the Wars of the Roses). In *Part Three* York is killed, but his clan win, and proclaim Edward king. Warwick captures Edward, who then escapes and with his brother, Richard, kills Margaret's son. Richard despatches Henry VI in the Tower and goes on, in *Richard III*, to be even more evil.

Henry IV Parts One and Two (1596–97) was first published in 1600 with bits missing, but was published complete in 1623. It starts with the Percy rebellion and Hotspur getting killed by Prince Hal. Northumberland and York rebel against Henry, meet his army led by Prince John at Gaultree Forest (Henry wasn't well that day), make peace, are promised a hearing, but are then executed. Henry, who is still ill, hears of the death of Northumberland, and gets worse and dies talking to his son, Prince Hal. Hal is then crowned Henry V.

> ### GROUNDLINGS' GOSSIP
>
> Overall the Histories cover the political events in England from 1398, when Richard II began to lose the plot, to 1485, when Richard III was defeated on Bosworth Field. *King John* is an exception because it is set in the 13th century. The Histories are sometimes called 'Chronicle' plays (though a 'chronicle' is really a specific type of history play), and it is fair to suggest Shakespeare invented the form.

> **DRAMATIS PERSONAE**
>
> American **Ignatius Donnelly** (1835–1901), denounced by some as the 'prince of crackpots', was convinced that he had found proof in Henry IV Parts One and Two that Francis Bacon wrote Shakespeare's plays.
>
> It was 'a long and continuous narrative running through, always growing from the same numbers [that formed] a prearranged arithmetical cipher' which more or less spelt out 'I, Francis Bacon, wrote these plays.' Good gracious, Ignatius!

1595 In England, Sir Philip Sydney publishes 'An Apologie for Poetrie'.

1599 The Duke of Lerma introduces copper coinage into Spain.

1601 English adventurer John Smith fights with Transylvania's Sigismund Báthory against the Turks, but is captured and sold into slavery.

1595~1613

The Histories: Part the Second
Richard II, King John, Henry V, Henry VIII

Richard II (1595) was first published in the First Quarto in 1597. Its primary source was Holinshed and it was first acted by the Lord Chamberlain's Men. It starts with a charge of treason brought by Bolingbroke against Thomas Mowbray, Duke of Norfolk. Richard exiles them both, then visits Bolingbroke's father, John of Gaunt. Gaunt tells him to grow up, stop spending too much and hanging around with idiots. So Richard waits for him to die (which he conveniently does) and impounds his estates. While Richard's away, various nobles, upset at his actions, side with Bolingbroke, who gets crowned as Henry IV. Richard is thrown in prison, and then bumped off.

King John (1596–97) is based on an earlier, anonymous, play called *The Troublesome Reign of John, King of England* and is set in the 13th century. King Philip of France, with John's nephew Prince Arthur, deny John's right to the throne, so John, with Philip Faulconbridge the bastard (by birth, I've nothing against him personally), invade France and kill Arthur. English nobles, angry with this, side with the French (with friends like these, who needs enemies?).

Derek Jacobi as Richard II using a stair to reinforce his status.

1608 Dutch lensmaker Hans Lippershey invents the refracting telescope.

1610 Ben Jonson's *The Alchemist* is performed for the first time; the prologue refers to 'Fortune that favours fools'.

1613 Londonderry is founded in Ulster as England gives 'plantations' of up to 3,000 acres each to Protestant settlers from England and Scotland.

'I saw him break Skogan's head.' *Henry IV Part One* (Act III, Scene 2)

DRAMATIS PERSONAE

Richard II *has been called Shakespeare's first tragedy because it analyzes the character of Richard as man as well as king. He is a weak man who listens to bad advice, makes bad decisions and* would therefore have been better employed as a writer!

Bringing the house down

Henry VIII had a very inauspicious start to its life. On 29 June 1613, during its first performance, a cannon, fired to announce the entrance of the king, announced the exit of the theatre instead. Its blast set fire to the thatched roof and the theatre was burned to the ground in one hour. There was only one casualty, however – a poor unfortunate whose trousers were set ablaze.

But Faulconbridge's troops beat the French, so the English nobles now desert the French. A monk finally poisons John, and everyone applauds. The key figure here is Faulconbridge who, despite (or even because of) being a bastard is a clear figure of heroism. *Henry V* (1599) was Shakespeare's ninth history play, and he may by then have got a bit tired of them. Henry tries to grab the throne of France through claim of lineal descent from Edward III. The French, being unreasonable, don't see it this way, so Henry invades. After his victory at Agincourt, Henry marries Katherine and gets the French king, Charles, to name him heir to France.

Henry VIII (1613), Shakespeare's last play, was probably co-written with John Fletcher. Henry marries Ann, and Cranmer predicts their daughter (Elizabeth) will rule England better than anyone before!

1590 The siege of Paris brings hunger and malnutrition that kill 13,000 in the city; the Spanish ambassador proposes grinding the bones of the dead to make flour.

1591 *The Troublesome Raigne of King John of English* is published anonymously, five years before Shakespeare writes his version.

1593 Purana Pul bridge with 23 arches is built across the River Musi in Hyberabad.

1590~1601

Disguises, Intrigue and a Bit of Cross-Dressing

A skirmish of wit in the Light Comedies

Dr Johnson commented that Shakespeare made his mark in comedy early because he was a naturally brilliant comic writer. Even his serious works have comic characters in them: imagine Hamlet without Polonius, Hal without Falstaff or even Macbeth without the Porter. His early comedy was unusual for its time, too. Whereas others satirized 'types', Will's lighter comedies get his audiences to laugh with the characters as well as at them, and he ends most with a reconciling marriage.

Actors playing Shylock were costumed and made up so that no one could fail to see the root of the 'problem'!

GROUNDLINGS' GOSSIP

In *The Merry Wives of Windsor*, Falstaff accuses Mistress Ford of 'carving', which was the gesture of raising and wiggling their little finger when drinking from a vessel. Unfortunately it was a signal favoured by whores to mean something along the lines of 'come and get it' to any man watching. Something the well-to-do ladies of today should bear in mind when sipping their tea!

Twelfth Night (1600–1601) is probably the best comedy, and *The Merchant of Venice* (1596) the most difficult – the 'Shylock' problem being famous for aggravating everyone. *The Comedy of Errors* (1590–93), *The Taming of the Shrew* (1592–93) and *The Merry Wives of Windsor* (1597) are the most 'classical' works, drawing directly from Terence and Plautus. They are mistaken-identity middle-class farces that are still popular

today. But they are not as robust in comic terms as the 'deceits' of *Love's Labours Lost* (1593), *Twelfth Night* or *Much Ado About Nothing* (1598–99). This last play also has scenes of serious drama within it that, like *The Merchant of Venice*, cast some doubt on how much it is a comedy at

1594 Queen Elizabeth I sends an organ, made by Thomas Dallas, to the Sultan of Turkey.

1598 Pueblo territory in the American Southwest is colonized by 400 Spanish men, women and children who arrive in more than 80 wagons with 7,000 head of livestock.

1601 Ben Jonson's play *Every Man in his Humour* premieres.

Falstaff of life

One fundamental distinction between Shakespeare's comedy and that of his fellow playwrights, especially neoclassicists such as Jonson or Molière, was that whereas the others appealed to the intellect and critical faculties, Shakespeare's comedy was emotional, fanciful and much more human. His Falstaff, for example, although a scruffy old lecher, is graced with wit, imagination and above all, vitality.

Falstaff and Robin heading for the bar.

(especially girls dressed as boys) as in *Twelfth Night*, *As You Like It* (1599–1600) and his first romantic comedy, *Two Gentlemen of Verona* (1592–93), have their roots in the plays of the Italian *commedia dell'arte* companies that visited England earlier in the century. Shakespeare used the intrigue plot of *I Suppositi*, by the Italian writer Ariosto, as a subplot of *The Taming of the Shrew*. But 'disguising' was also a favourite pastime of courtiers, pursued with glee as part of the many pageants and masques they attended. Dressing up was very popular because it allowed a degree of flirtation protected by anonymity. In fact, John Dover Wilson has noted that 'To make love, or be made love to, *masked*, was one of the principal sports of the age…'. Here is a pleasure still enjoyed today, although usually within certain private clubs patronized by judges, politicians and chiefs of police.

all, and substantiate the arguments of those who believe that both plays should be classed as Problem Plays *(see page 74)*.

The device of 'intrigue' and the use of disguise in Shakespeare's comedies

John Gielgud and Diane Wynyard in *Much Ado About Nothing* at the Phoenix Theatre in 1952.

1601 Thomas Middleton writes his play *Blurt, Master Constable.*

1602 Spanish traders arrive in Japan.

1603 A Sikh shrine, the Golden Temple at Amritsar in the Punjab, is completed, with its copper dome and walls and cupola covered in gold foil.

1601~1604
The Problem Plays
Or, Mr Shakespeare gets crabby

Troilus and Cressida *(1601–1602),* All's Well That Ends Well *(1602–1603)* and Measure For Measure *(1604) represent a return to comedy for Shakespeare, but of a different kind. Here a bitter, sardonic feeling enters the writing, for reasons we can only guess at. Shakespeare may have been experimenting with the comic genre (they are also known as the Dark Comedies), may have been influenced by Jonson, or both. Or maybe it was just a case of 'No more Mr Nice Guy'.*

T*roilus* has irritated scholars a lot – mainly because they can't seem to establish when, where and how it was first performed. Ah, the cruel mysteries of life! Troilus and Cressida are in love, but she

The RSC's 1993 production of *All's Well That Ends Well.*

The RSC's *Troilus and Cressida* (1996) found ingenious ways for actors to take up less space.

plays it too cool, and ends up mistress to someone else. Troilus vows to kill the other man, but doesn't – and, er, that's about it. To those who see the play as a comedy, Shakespeare is attacking military heroes and revealing them as weak and proud. And the notion of 'romantic love' takes a beating, since Elizabethans would have considered Cressida little more than a fickle tart.

All's Well That Ends Well, based on 14th-century Boccaccio's *Decameron,* revolves around Helena, an orphan, who loves Bertram. He agrees to marriage, but disappears to France, then writes to her stipulating that she can only be his wife if

1603 Platt makes coke from coal by heating it without air and therefore providing a pure carbon – ideal for smelting.

1603 The Tokugawa shogunate is established in Edo (Tokyo).

1604 Italian painter Caravaggio completes *The Deposition*.

she can do two things: get a ring off his finger, and become pregnant with his child – but while he remains in France! With a bit of trickery, she succeeds (see the play to find out how) and they reunite. But it wasn't a popular comedy; the earliest known performance was 1741 and it only gained some regard in the 20th century.

Isabella questions Angelo about the deal he made, in *Measure for Measure*.

Measure for Measure centres even more on sex, from the brothel to the nunnery. The unpleasantness of its subject-matter and the complexity of its plot and themes have been the source of much debate among Bardophiles. Its tone is dark and moralistic in that, as its title suggests,

Don't pander to me!

The story of Troilus and Cressida was well known to Elizabethans (Chaucer, for one, had already done it), so much so that by the time Shakespeare's play was staged, it was common to refer to all 'good, true lovers' as Troiluses, and all 'false women' as Cressidas. The character of Pandarus was similarly familiar – all 'Panders' were procurers!

a sense of 'measure' ('moderation') is equated with a healthy lifestyle. It is also alone among Shakespeare's plays in the sheer number of strange and bizarre images it conjures up. For example, 'liberty plucks justice by the nose', or it may 'make him bite the law by the nose'; while Lucio says of Claudio, *'Thy head stands so tickle on thy shoulders that a milkmaid, if she be in love, may sign it off.'* But it is a comedy nevertheless, and very bawdy, too, in parts. Angelo orders the closing of all brothels in Vienna, and sentences Claudio to death for making Angelo's fiancée pregnant. Claudio's sister, Isabella, a nun, pleads for his life, so Angelo agrees to free Claudio if he can have sex with Isabella! Do you think he manages it?

GROUNDLINGS' GOSSIP

The character with the most unfortunate name in *Troilus and Cressida* is poor Ajax. Shakespeare has him called 'melancholy without cause', 'a stool for a witch' and 'a thing of no bowels'. Which must have caused much mirth, because of Sir John Harington's book, *The Metamorphosis of Ajax* published in 1596, proposing the introduction of the flush lavatory ('a jax'). This book had Harington exiled from court.

1606 In Canada a performance of *La Theatre de Neptune en la Nouvelle-France* at Port Royal is one of the first plays to be staged in the New World.

1607 English playwrights Beaumont and Fletcher pen *The Knight of the Burning Pestle,* the first of 50 comedies and tragedies that the two will write together.

1609 English explorer Henry Hudson reaches New York Bay and sails up the river which now takes his name.

1606~1611

The Last Plays
Will's just an old softy after all

The four 'Last Plays' – Pericles, Cymbeline, The Winter's Tale *and* The Tempest *(see page 62) – are Shakespeare's final works, written in the years just before he ultimately retired to Stratford, the wife and rose-pruning. They are sometimes termed 'the Romances', and are categorized in this way because they are neither tragedy nor comedy, but have some elements of both. But they are not 'tragicomedies' either – because that term implies an equal measure of both. They are, according to Alfred Harbage, comedies with 'tragic potential' (someone once told me I was 'tragic' but I don't think it's the same thing).*

In all these plays evil is present but is denied any form of triumph. The sins of the older generation are swept aside by younger, brighter aspirations, and rejuvenation and renewal, often with a touch of magic, are recurrent themes. Techniques Shakespeare learned from earlier plays are here employed to create a world where characters' actions are determined more by personal compulsion, or chance, or the heavens than by any act of choice. And there is plenty of death, missing-presumed-dead intrigue and,

just to keep it in the family, a bit of incest. In *Pericles* (1606–1608), the Prince of Tyre finds his life in danger after he solves a riddle that reveals incest between King Antiochus and his daughter, so he runs away. He marries, but his wife dies in childbirth.

Cymbeline, in the RSC's 1997 production, spots Imogen's wedding ring. Oops.

1609 Portugal takes Ceylon (Sri Lanka) from the Dutch.

1610 Galileo publishes *The Starry Messenger*, describing the Milky Way and the moons of Jupiter.

1610 The Dutch East India Company introduces the concept of 'shares'.

Posthumus love

These plays don't have as many images running through them as most of the others, which has caused some fanatics to claim he didn't write them (what doesn't?). But they contain some of the most beautiful motifs. One such is that of remorse, in *Cymbeline*, where Posthumus, as Imogen throws her arms round him in forgiveness, murmurs, 'Hang there like fruit, my soul, Till the tree die!'

Pericles taking baby Marina and moving house.

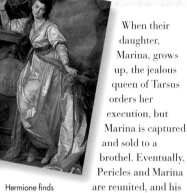

Hermione finds herself in *The Winter's Tale*, by Zoffany (1780).

When their daughter, Marina, grows up, the jealous queen of Tarsus orders her execution, but Marina is captured and sold to a brothel. Eventually, Pericles and Marina are reunited, and his wife magically appears in the temple of Diana!

Cymbeline (1609–10) is based on an early British legend of King Cymbeline who banishes his daughter Imogen's secret husband, Posthumus. There then follows a great deal of intrigue and disguising and some fighting with Rome. At the end it's reconciliation all round. This play wasn't very popular in its time, nor has it been staged much since.

The Winter's Tale (1611) is based on a prose romance, *Pandosto, or the Triumph of Time*, by Robert Greene (a certain irony there). It concerns King Leontes, who

GROUNDLINGS' GOSSIP

Pericles was printed in 1609 in a corrupt text, but is the only one of Shakespeare's plays omitted from the 1623 Folio edition. It is generally believed that the first two acts are by another playwright, with Shakespeare taking over at the point where the story caught his imagination – and completing acts III, IV and V.

suspects his wife, Hermione, of having an affair with King Polixenes. He orders death all round, and, when Hermione gives birth to a girl he's convinced isn't his, he orders wife and daughter killed, too. But neither Hermione nor the child, Perdita, die. Instead, after much lamenting and repenting, all are re-united, as the original title 'the Triumph of Time' tells us.

1595 Famine brings unrest and peasant revolt to Austria, but food is available in Vienna at inflated prices.

1601 In England, Queen Elizabeth gives her famous 'Golden Speech' to Parliament.

1603 Johan Bayer's astronomical atlas 'Uranometria' maps out 12 new southern constellations and, for the first time, groups stars according to their luminosity.

1592~1609

Long Poems and Sexy Sonnets
Iambic pentameter... is that a new computer?

Adonis is killed by a boar

In addition to his plays, Shakespeare also penned narrative poems – Venus and Adonis (1593) and The Rape of Lucrece *(1594) – A Lover's Complaint (a poem in rhyme royal appended to the Sonnets) and probably* The Phoenix and the Turtle, *as well as his 154 sonnets. Thomas Thorpe first published the sonnets, probably against Shakespeare's wishes. There is much speculation as to when the sonnets were written, but since the dates offered by 'experts' range from 1592 to 1606 we needn't waste much time on that! Of much more interest is the story they tell.*

A sonnet is a verse of 14 rhymed iambic pentameter lines. And an iambic pentameter is a sort of rhythm where each line goes de-*da*, de-*da*, de-*da*, de-*da*, de-*da*, with the accent on the '*da*'. For example, the first two lines of Sonnet 30 run thus:

'*When to the sessions of sweet silent thought*
I summon up remembrance of things past.'

Secret sonnets

It was possible Shakespeare took such a keen interest in his sonnets, and in ensuring a solid patron for his career, because the theatres were closed in 1592–93 by the plague (over 10,000 people died that year, in a city of 200,000). It's also possible, however, that they were never intended for the public eye.

'Lucrece,' quoth he, 'this night I must enjoy thee:

If thou deny, then force must work my way. '

1609 Johannes Kepler develops his first two laws of planetary motion.

1607 A third English East India Company fleet sails in March for the Indies and will return with cloves and other cargo yielding an enormous profit.

1608 Thomas Middleton writes *A Mad World My Masters*.

An imagined representation of the Youth of the Sonnets. Puhleese!

ost lust

hakespeare always ad a few salient ords to say about the fference between ve and lust. In *Venus nd Adonis*, stanza 33, he says, 'Love's entle spring doth ways fresh remain, / st's winter comes ere mmer half be done; / Love surfeits not, Lust ke a glutton dies; / ove is all truth, Lust ll of forged lies.' And n't that just the truth!

The rhythm is clear when spoken out loud. The Shakespearean sonnet rhymes thus: abab, cdcd, efef, gg (where each letter stands for a line and all lines with the same letter are supposed to rhyme).

Venus and Adonis is a romantic poem, and was actually Shakespeare's most popular work during his lifetime – probably because of its bawdiness. Inspired by Ovid's *Metamorphoses*, it tells of the

doomed romance between two beautiful, but rather dim, lovers. Like *Lucrece*, it is dedicated to his patron, Henry Wriothesley, the Earl of Southampton, a young nobleman also assumed to be the subject of many of the sonnets. *The Rape of Lucrece*, a far more sombre affair, is about the rape of poor Lucrece by one Tarquin after her stupid husband, Collatinus, wins a bragging contest about how virtuous she is. She eventually kills herself and Tarquin and his entire family are exiled from Rome.

GROUNDLINGS' GOSSIP

A collection of 20 poems, called *The Passionate Pilgrim* 'By W. Shakespeare', was printed in 1599. But they weren't all his, because the stationer, William Jaggard, had used Shakespeare's name without permission. At Shakespeare's insistence, his name was removed from the front cover.

1596 Sir Francis Drake dies of the dysentry at sea in the West Indies, near the town of Nombre de Dios.

1598 Spanish artist El Greco paints *St. Martin and the Beggar*.

1601 Queen Elizabeth punishes her previous favourite the Earl of Essex for his failure in Ireland and finally puts him on trial.

1592~1609

Was the Bard Playing on, er, Both Sides?

The Poet, the Dark Lady and a Rather Attractive Youth

Some of Shakespeare's sonnets and poems have fascinated biographers, for it appears he was writing most of them to a young man, and the rest to a 'Dark Lady'. Given the expressions of 'love' for both parties in the sonnets, various critics and writers, including Oscar Wilde, have suggested he was either a) homosexual, b) bisexual, c) a womanizer or d) all three. No wonder his handwriting was shaky!

The Dark Lady herself! Mary Fitton looking suitably exotic and alluring.

Shakespeare's patron, Henry Wriothesley. Was he the Youth?

The first 126 sonnets seem to be addressed to an attractive youth, and are dedicated to a 'W.H.'. In them Shakespeare expresses affection and admiration for the young man, though he does suggest he marry and have children. Most of the remaining sonnets are addressed to the notorious Dark Lady, with dark hair and eyes. No one knows for sure who these people might have been, although the woman is believed to have been one Mary Fitton, Maid of Honour at Court (who bore three illegitimate children). In the 1960s historian A.L. Rowse proposed that she was Emilia Lanier, daughter of a court musician. From the initials W.H., it is thought the youth was either Henry Wriothesley, Earl of Southampton and Shakespeare's only patron, or William

---

GROUNDLINGS' GOSSIP

As to what Shakespeare was up to in his private life, so many questions remain unanswered. For a start, it seems he never allowed his wife and children to live with him in London, possibly not even to visit him. Why should this be so? Certainly the London he lived in was more corrupt then than at any time since. Or it might have been that he just wanted the freedom of bachelorhood again.

1603 The first beaver skins arrive in the French port of La Rochelle from Canada.

1605 Caravaggio's painting *Death of Madonna* (commissioned for Santa Maria della Scala, Travastere) is rejected on grounds of indecency as the swollen body is said to look as though it belongs to a poor person.

1607 Sir Thomas Smith establishes the first successful English settlement in North America at Jamestown, Virginia.

Herbert, Earl of Pembroke. But Wriothesley's initials, of course, are the wrong way round, and although Pembroke's initials fit, he was only about 14 years old when the sonnets were written, too young for marriage. (My own theory is that Shakespeare, the family man, was dedicating them to his good 'Wife Hathaway', but there is not a *shred* of evidence to support this.)

Extracts from the sonnets give us some idea of the problem in hand. In Sonnet 17, he wrote to the youth 'If I could write the

DRAMATIS PERSONAE

Shakespeare was not responsible for publication of his sonnets. By some means, Thomas Thorpe, a procurer of manuscripts, was able to secure them. With no copyright laws, once the manuscripts were in his possession, he could do what he wanted with them. He commissioned George Eld to print them and John Wright and William Aspley, booksellers, sold them for 'fivepence'.

beauty of your eyes / And in fresh numbers, number all your graces'. Describing the 'Dark Lady' in Sonnet 127 he wrote 'In the old age black was not counted fair, / Or if it were, it bore not beauty's name; / But now is black beauty's successive heir.... / Therefore my mistress' eyes are raven black'. In Sonnet 130 he added: 'If snow be white, why then her breasts are dun; / If hairs be wires, black wires grow on her head.'

Silly Willy

That Shakespeare actually *wrote* the sonnets is evidenced, some think, in sonnets 135, 136 and 143. The key is the word 'will'. In Sonnet 135 'will' is capitalized in places, and 'For my name is Will,' is the way that Sonnet 136 ends. This and the lousy spelling prove it must have been he!

Shakespeare in love? Joseph Fiennes as the Bard in John Madden's Oscar-winning film.

1586 In York, Margaret Clitheroe is pressed to death for hiding priests.

1587 Sir Francis Drake captures the Spanish treasure ship *Sao Felipe* and claims her cargo of bullion, silks, spices, Chinese porcelains, pearls and gemstones.

1589 English clergyman William Lee invents the first knitting machine; Elizabeth refuses to grant a patent for his stocking frame so he sets up his frames in Rouen, France.

1550~1642

Here Come the Puritans…Look Miserable!

Moral objections to acting, laughing and living

An Elizabethan play in performance – before the Puritans sent everyone home.

Throughout Shakespeare's days there were two forces opposing theatre and entertainment generally in London: the Puritans, those Protestant crusaders dedicated to promoting 'godly discipline' among the sinners of Babylon, and the London Aldermen, who blamed the theatre for luring the 'prentices and servants of the City from their works'. In 1597, the Aldermen, endorsed by the Privy Council, petitioned for the 'final suppression of stage plays'. The companies were only saved by royal patronage, whereby it was accepted that some 'licence' was necessary for the health of the community. As Shakespeare later declared in Twelfth Night, *'There is no slander in an allowed fool'.*

These forces had already exiled theatre outside of the city walls, but the 'evil' was spreading, and the sin of make-believe was popping up everywhere! Puritan opposition to this, of course, was fuelled by pure envy. Theatre was popular, theatres were full: the church, however, was neither. Fortunately,

Cheap sheets

In 1632, when the second Folio collection was published in Will's honour, the Puritans whined that 'Schackspeere's plaies are printed in the best crowne paper, far better than most Bibles'. Between 1631 and 1633, 40,000 playbooks were bought. One wonders whether sermon sheets were in similar demand.

Elizabeth was unimpressed by these zealots and gave theatre royal assent (without which Shakespeare might never had a play performed).

By 1602 the Corporation of London, made up of Puritans and Aldermen, decided that 'there shall be no plays or interludes played in the Chamber, the Guild

1592 Christopher Marlowe's *The Tragicall History of Dr Faustus* is produced for the first time, about the man who sold his soul to the Devil.

1620 A group of Puritans sets sail for Massachussetts aboard the *Mayflower* to set up a strict religious community.

1638 Japanese Christianity is wiped out in the Shimabar uprising.

Hall, nor in any part of the House or Court from henceforward'. Any official who gave permission should be fined 10 shillings (about a week's wages for a successful merchant), and by 1612 this fine was increased to £10! But the need for entertainment was as great as ever, and plays were still performed around the country.

Charles I at a cock fight. It's not known whether he had any money on one of the birds, but I hope not – I get the feeling that he's just not going to get lucky.

Eventually, however, the Puritans slowly gained the upper hand, and, in 1622, even Shakespeare's old company, the King's Men, were paid 6 shillings for *not* performing at the Guildhall in the Midlands. In later years they performed exclusively at Blackfriars and Whitehall, as public theatre disappeared. Theatre after Charles I degenerated into 'cavalier' dramas written by poor writers for the bimbo Queen Henrietta and her ladies at court, so becoming merely an aristocratic diversion. In 1642, Parliament decreed that 'public stage plays shall cease and be forborne', and theatres remained closed for 18 years (by then theatre in England had had it anyway).

> ## GROUNDLINGS' GOSSIP
>
> Worse than 'pretending' was the heinous crime of *storytelling*. One Puritan, Stephen Gosson, warned earnestly that 'plays are the invention of the devil, the offerings of idolatry... the food of iniquity', and that the actors were 'masters of vice, teachers of wantonness...' (probably the best review some of them ever got).

As You Like It, staged in the yard of an inn. From an engraving by Joseph Swain.

1660 In Britain, tea – by now a fashionable medicinal drink – becomes subject to tax for the first time.

1664 French painter Nicolas Poussin, now over 70, puts the finishing touches to his painting *Apollo and Daphne*.

1666 The first Turnpike Act is passed in Britain allowing tolls to be charged for road usage.

1660~1685
The Boys Are Back in Town!
Let's get this show back on the road

The return of Charles II to Whitehall in 1660.

In 1646, four years after Charles I left Parliament and the Civil War started, the Globe theatre was demolished to make way for tenement housing. In 1660 Charles II reclaimed the throne and by his sanction the theatre was kick-started into life once more. There had been a few surreptitious performances in between, but Will's plays had not been published since 1632, and people had largely forgotten him (not so much through short memory-span as short life-span). Even the hundreds of manuscripts he must have written or signed had been mostly lost.

Charles II granted patents to give two new companies, the King's Company (at the Theatre Royal, which became the Drury Lane theatre) and the Duke of York's Company (at the Salisbury Court theatre), a monopoly on staging dramas in London. This lasted 183 years! These theatres also employed actresses such as Nell Gwynne, Anne Bracegirdle and Elizabeth Barry. Sir William Davenant, who managed the Duke's Company, had, as a boy, known Shakespeare (Davenant was rumoured to be Shakespeare's bastard son). So he was instrumental in reviving the Shakespeare canon on stage. He taught one of his actors, Thomas Betterton, to become a great player of Shakespeare's tragic roles.

The lovely and charmingly named Anne Bracegirdle.

Women's parts
Shakespeare's plays were rewritten to accommodate actresses. Nahum Tate adapted many, including *King Lear*, in which he had Edgar in love with Cordelia (whereas in fact they never even spoke to each other!). He justified it by saying that her love for Edgar explained why she was so indifferent to her father's wishes in the first scene (Shakespeare obviously overlooked that possibility).

1670 A scientist called Willis shows that the condition diabetes makes the sufferer's urine sweet.

1667 At the Royal Society, London, Robert Boyle demonstrates artificial respiration on a dog.

1684 A Dutch tailor creates the first thimble after pricking his thumb one time too many.

Davenant also introduced moving scenery and painted wings. Prior to this Shakespeare's plays had been lavishly costumed, but on stages fairly devoid of props or scenery. Now Davenant's insistence on using scenery altered the way Shakespeare's work was perceived.

Drama became more 'upper class' to survive, and so did Shakespeare. The clientele changed – even the King loved going to the theatre, and when in London went every day (he also took actress Nell Gwynne as a lover – the first, but certainly not last, thespian social climber). As Shakespearean scholar Gary Taylor puts it: 'Before 1642 the plays went to the monarch; after 1660 the monarch went to plays.'

GROUNDLINGS' GOSSIP

Actresses appeared on the English stage at the same time as pornography. This represented a double bonus for men. All Samuel Pepys could say about a certain actress was that she had the 'very best legs that ever I saw; and I was very well plesed'. As well as viewing female flesh on stage, he also bought a translation of *L'escholle des Filles*, read it, masturbated and burned it!

There were other 'minor' theatres that had permission to put on short plays (plays that were no more than four acts long), operas, melodramas, pantomimes and concerts. So Shakespeare's works were sometimes reduced and turned into operas. *John DRYDEN* (1631–1700) wrote *All For Love* in 1678, a condensed version of *Antony and Cleopatra*. And, hard though it is to believe, *Macbeth* and *The Tempest* were transformed into very successful musicals! But gradually, Shakespeare's plays became more widely known and became regular inclusions in the new 'repertoire' idea in the patented theatres.

Rymer the whiner
The first English drama critic, Thomas Rymer, began his career in 1674. But he didn't include Shakespeare in his critical gaze until 1693 in *A Short View of Tragedy*. Of course, he didn't think too much of him, complaining among other things about Othello's calling for 'a huge Eclipse / Of Sun and Moon' together. Not possible he whined.

Mark Rylance and Paul Shelley in *Antony and Cleopatra*.

1689 Henry Purcell writes the first British opera, *Dido and Aeneas*.

1701 Detroit is founded in the United States by Antoine de Cadillac.

1714 Jethro Tull develops a horse-drawn hoe, described in his book *Horse Hoeing Husbandry*.

1685~1750

The Ghastly Middle Classes
From William and Mary to the Great Garrick

Charles II had loved the theatre, and his death, in 1685, marked another decline for the dramatic arts, as for much else. His successor, James II, was anything but successful. He upset the country so much he provoked the Glorious Revolution of 1688, and then gave the throne to William and Mary, the po-faced Protestant Pairs of Pursed Lips. The Moralists were back – and this time they were hopping mad!

A cartoon of *Henry IV* in production. But where are the speech bubbles?

Highland fling
Macbeth, staged at Drury Lane in 1726, featured 'Songs, Dances and Other decorations proper to the play…[such as] a Wooden Shoe Dance by Mr. Sandham's Children…the 8th of Corelli's Concertos [and]…La Peirette by Mr Roger the Peiror and Mrs Brent'.

The best dramatists of the Restoration period were either dead or very old, and new blood was slow to flow. The climate was less than welcoming. A pamphlet, *Immorality, and Profaneness of the English Stage*, by Jeremy Collier, was reprinted three times in 1698. Daniel Defoe described a performance of *Henry IV* at Oxford as '*full of profane, immoral, and some blasphemous Parts… Is not Religion*

banter'd in it, the Church ridicul'd..?' Actors wished he would disappear to his desert island. By 1698 there was talk of closing the theatres down again.

In 1693 Christopher Rich, a moneylender, took over Davenant's company, ousting Shakespeare in favour of light entertainment for quick profit. At Drury Lane he ruined the acoustics by pushing the stage back to add boxes to increase his income. Theatre lost the intimacy of Shakespeare's day, and became duller and more middle-class. In 1709 complaints by actors closed Drury Lane, but it reopened in 1710 under Colley Cibber and two actor-managers.

1737 David Garrick sets out with his teacher, the lexicographer Samuel Johnson, on a journey to London.

1732 Benjamin Franklin's popular *Poor Richard's Almanack* appears for the first time.

1749 London cabinet-maker Thomas Chippendale opens a factory to make furniture.

Shakespeare's tragedies proved popular during the early 18th century, mainly because there weren't any others worth staging, except perhaps those of *Nicholas ROWE* (1674–1718). But his comedies were eclipsed by those of Dryden, Vanbrugh, Congreve, Farquhar, Gay and Cibber himself. Thomas Betterton died in 1710, and until Garrick appeared there was no actor able to fill his boots. Cibber was a good comedy actor, but most other 'stars' of the time were little more than hams.

David GARRICK (1717–79) was the best Shakespearean actor of his age, and, from 1747, the best manager Drury Lane had ever seen. But, like many others, he couldn't leave the Bard's work alone. He added a dying speech to *Macbeth*, took the gravediggers out of *Hamlet* (and rewrote the end), and, in his 1748 production of *Romeo and Juliet*, Juliet wakes up and has a 65-line chat with Romeo!

Spranger Barry and Miss Nossiter as Romeo and Juliet – hardly teenage lovers!

GROUNDLINGS' GOSSIP

And here's a most appropriate finale to *Othello* (Drury Lane, 1764). He's just strangled his wife, then stabbed himself, but they thought it fit to add 'a Double Hornpipe...a dance called "The Carpenters and The Fruit Dealers"...and a new Epilogue... followed by "The Witches: or Harlequin Cherokee"'.

David Garrick as Richard III, by William Hogarth (1745).

1754 St Petersburg's Winter Palace is completed by the Italian architect Bartolomeo Rastrelli.

1755 After eight years of work, lexicographer Samuel Johnson publishes his *Dictionary of the English Language*.

1756 123 of 146 British captives die after a night's imprisonment in a small, underground room known as the 'Black Hole of Calcutta'.

1750~1900

The Smell of Blood, and the Flash of Lightning!

Shakespeare in the hands of the Great and the Drunk

Things improved for the Bard as the 18th century progressed. Although the Licensing Act of 1737, continuing the monopoly created by the Royal Patents, limited legal playhouses to Covent Garden, Drury Lane and the Haymarket and made all other theatres illegal, this was typically ignored, and theatre flourished once more, albeit a different sort of theatre: indoor, lit by gas lamps and part of an entertainment 'package'. Some of the more outrageous additions to Shakespeare's work were finally removed, and the theatre's reviving fortunes promised a better supply of talented actors and producers.

'I smell blood!' Mrs Siddons sleepwalking through *Macbeth*.

During this period, however, there emerged a tendency to 'idealize' Shakespeare's words, thus furthering the cause of Bardolatry. Two acting schools evolved that had different ideas about how the Great Man's words should be properly interpreted. The first of these adopted the neoclassical style practised by *John Philip KEMBLE* (1757–1823) and his sister Sarah Siddons; the second, which developed after the turn of the century, espoused the more realistic approach of *Edmund KEAN* (1787–1833).

Siddons was so convincing as a sleepwalking Lady Macbeth, she prompted critic Sheridan Knowles to declare 'I smelt blood! I swear I smelt blood!' *George Frederick COOKE* (1756–1811), late 18th-century Covent Garden star, was considered to be Kemble's only

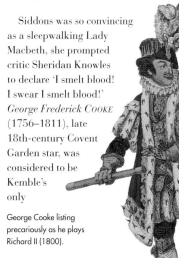

George Cooke listing precariously as he plays Richard II (1800).

1839 The British steeplechase, the Grand National, is held for the first time.

1854 By now Europe has 22,530 km (14,000 miles) of railway lines connecting most of the major cities.

1898 Russian actor-producer Konstantin Stanislavsky founds the Moscow Art Theatre and mounts a successful production of Chekhov's *The Seagull*.

DRAMATIS PERSONAE

Ex-Covent Garden tragedian **James Fennell** *(1766–1816) visited America and became a great success on his arrival in Philadelphia in 1792, playing major roles such as Othello and Lear.* **Thomas Abthorpe Cooper** *(1776–1849) was judged to be an excellent Macbeth at the Chestnut Street theatre in Philadelphia. In 1801 he moved to the Park Street theatre in New York, and five years later came to play a part in its management.*

serious rival. He specialized in several roles, including Richard III, Shylock, Iago and Sir Giles Overreach, but he drank too much and fell down a lot. Kean, who expended as much energy in the bedroom and bar as he did on stage (he had previously been referred to by Mrs Siddons as a 'horrid little man'), made a stunning London debut as Shylock in 1814. His career was great, but his short life was to end in drink and misery, as he collapsed on stage at 44. He had revolutionized acting by famously 'realistic' transitions from 'low' to 'high' in his delivery, causing Coleridge to comment that watching Kean was like 'reading Shakespeare by flashes of lightning'.

Edmund Kean looking shifty as Shylock, Drury Lane, 1814.

Political interference

Richard Brinsley Sheridan wrote comedies, such as *The Rivals* (1775), *A School For Scandal* (1777) and *The Critic; or A Tragedy Rehearsed* (1779), but grew more interested in political fame. He had bought Drury Lane in 1776, but it fell into disrepair. It reopened in 1794, however, and, with the help of Mrs Siddons and John Philip Kemble, flourished.

During the 18th century, many English actors toured America, despite the Puritan influence at work there too. Thomas Kean and William Murray toured Philadelphia successfully with their company in 1749, and opened *Richard III* in New York in 1750 with Kean playing the leading role. William Hallam's company opened *The Merchant of Venice* at Williamsburg in 1752.

GROUNDLINGS' GOSSIP

One of the many 'drunk' stories about George Cooke has it that, while playing Richard III in London, he staggered into the theatre one night to be accosted by the theatre manager who shouted, 'Mr. Cooke! You are drunk!' Cooke sneered at him, 'Drunk? Me drunk? Ha! You should see Buckingham!'

1787 The Marylebone Cricket Club is formed and the rules of the game are formally drawn up.

1793 King Louis XVI and Marie Antoinette of France are guillotined in Paris.

1806 Jane and Ann Taylor's *Rhymes for the Nursery* is one of the first collections of children's nursery rhymes.

1776~1835

What Do You Mean, the Ink's Still Wet?

William Henry Ireland, forger extraordinaire

I suppose one of the consequences of idolatry – or Bardolatry – is that there will always be those only too ready to produce 'found' objects for the faithful to worship. Mostly such objects are 'found' after the finder has spent hours in a locked den. So it was with one of the most famous forgers of Shakespeareana, William Henry IRELAND (1776–1835).

Ireland, as a 19-year-old lawyer's clerk, produced an amazing number of Shakespearean 'finds', including a complete new 'lost' play, *Vortigern*. He also 'found' letters supposedly sent between Shakespeare and his patron, the Earl of Southampton; documents declaring his allegiance to the Protestant faith; (bad) drawings by him; a letter to him from Elizabeth I; and a truly terrible poem to one 'Anna Hatherrewaye'. In all these forgeries he maintained, even expanded, an 'Elizabethan style' of spelling which was erratic to the point of ridiculousness. Yet he fooled rich and famous alike.

Vorti-gone

The performance of *Vortigern* on 2 April 1796 attracted an audience of 2,500. Richard Brinsley Sheridan, who managed the theatre then, had accepted it in contract. All went well until Act V, when John Philip Kemble delivered the line, *'And when this solemn mockery is o'er'*, in 'sepulchral tones'. The audience roared at what they now realized was a pile of rubbish, and howled it off stage.

1812 The Gas Light and Coke Company is formed in London and uses gas street lighting for the first time, on Westminster Bridge.

1815 Kelp prices collapse in Scotland.

1847 The opera *Macbeth* by Giuseppe Verdi opens in Italy.

False accounts

There had been forgeries of Shakespeare's work circulating as early as 1595, when a play entitled *Locrine* was wrongly attributed to him. In the 1850s, John Payne Collier, a scholar, took to 'amending' Shakespeare's works, and a decade later, one retired employee of the Records Office by the name of Peter Cunningham offered up the account books of the Revels Office for the years 1604–1605 and 1610–11; they were also falsified.

Pile 'em high, sell 'em cheap! *Coriolanus* at Drury Lane Theatre (by Pugin and A.F. Rowlandson). Hard to believe Coriolanus was ever as popular as that!

Part of his initial success can be attributed to a proliferation of forgers during the latter part of the 17th century. Bardolatry had shifted into a higher gear after Cibber, Garrick and others had rediscovered the Old Boy, and 'new' finds were often not inspected too closely. This was good news for Mr Ireland, because his forgeries were not very good. Early success with small fraud prompted him to bigger and better things, such as 'finding' a copy of the '*Tragedye of Kynge Leare*' and a few pages from '*Hamblette*'. He also created a letter, supposedly written by Shakespeare, which served as a lease agreement for Shakespeare's Blackfriars house with a previously unknown 'ancestor' of his – also, by coincidence, called William Henry Ireland.

John Philip Kemble as *Coriolanus*. So bold!

> ### GROUNDLINGS' GOSSIP
>
> Shakespeareana was very collectable, but in any case William Ireland's father, Samuel, was one of the most diligent collectors of anything. He reputedly owned Shakespeare's 'courting chair', a First Folio, hair from the head of Edward IV and Louis XVI, Oliver Cromwell's leather jacket and a purse given to Henry VIII by Anne Boleyn.

1789 George Washington becomes the first president of the US.

1857 Civil divorce becomes possible in Britain for the first time.

1860 Newnham invents the press-stud fastener.

1780~1900
Bill Hits the Big Time
The Bard and Victorian values

Shakespeare's influence on 19th-century writers was very great and not always good. Wordsworth, Byron, Shelley and Tennyson all attempted poetic drama, but they were terrible because they were more interested in becoming a second set of Shakespeares than in creating something new and fresh. The 'Shakespearean poetic play', wrote Allardyce Nicoll, was now 'the greatest hindrance to the development of prose drama'.

English theatre was becoming more and more respectable, and Shakespeare a figure of *literature*! William MACREADY (1793–1873), actor-manager of both Covent Garden and Drury Lane, exerted great influence on Victorian attitudes to Shakespeare, mixing 'naturalism' with high emotion. Charles Kean, the actor-son of Edmund, mounted productions marked more by ego than talent. *A Midsummer Night's Dream*, in 1856, lavishly set in Periclean Athens, was performed by characters better suited to a Christmas pantomime than a magic wood, and to make matters worse, his expensive and

'It wasn't me! It was my brother!' Edwin Booth as Iago.

showy productions unfortunately established certain expectations for the audiences of Shakespearean drama. No longer was it possible to set the Bard's work simply, giving full rein to action and audience imagination – massive staging resources became essential. The end of the century was dominated by Henry Irving at the Lyceum (1878–1901), and by Herbert Beerbohm Tree at the Haymarket (1887–96). Both actor-managers took their Shakespeare productions very seriously – almost as seriously as they took themselves. But eventually such elaborate, spectacular productions began to decline, especially after the drawing of the Swan

Maître d'hump
In 1821 an amateur company of free blacks performed *Richard III* in the African Grove, Manhattan. The head waiter at the Park Hotel played Richard, by all accounts wearing a costume made from curtains taken from the hotel dining-room.

1870 The first performances of Tchaikovsky's *Romeo and Juliet Overture (Fantasia after Shakespeare)* take place in Moscow.

1880 British cricketer W.G. Grace scores the first-ever test century in a match against Australia.

1886 In the US the dedication ceremony takes place for the Statue of Liberty, presented to America by the people of France.

theatre was discovered in 1888. Designers started reappraising the naked stage and the power of an audience's imagination, just as Shakespeare himself had suggested in his prologues!

Happily Shakespeare was extremely popular in America by now, as he was in Germany and Europe (his work was published in most European countries from the mid 1700s). Many good lessons in interpretation and staging came from overseas, often learned by English actors who frequently travelled abroad (sometimes at the request of English audiences!).

In America, *Edwin BOOTH* (1833–93) staged many excellent Shakespearean productions between 1869 and 1874 at his own theatre in New York. Charlotte Cushman toured Britain in the mid-century and wowed audiences with her Lady Macbeth and Romeo (her sister played Juliet). *James HACKETT* (1800–71) played Falstaff to great acclaim in New York. From Italy in the 1860s and 1870s came Tomasso Salvini and Ernesto Rossi, performing to great acclaim as Hamlet, Othello, Lear and in other tragic roles.

DRAMATIS PERSONAE

While playing *Richard III*, Junius Brutus Booth, father of Edwin (and of John Wilkes Booth who shot Abraham Lincoln), apparently once fought the actor playing Richmond off the stage and into the orchestra pit. He then chased him down the aisles, through the foyer and out into the street, where his opponent cried submission. Booth threw down his sword and headed for the nearest bar.

Herbert Beerbohm Tree, glowering as Macbeth.

GROUNDLINGS' GOSSIP

The touring Miln Company performed *Hamlet, The Merchant of Venice, Macbeth, Othello, Romeo and Juliet, Julius Caesar* and *Richard II* at the Yokohama Public Hall in 1891. These were the first touring productions of Shakespeare's plays to go to Japan, although there had been a kabuki adaptation of *The Merchant of Venice* at the Osaka Ebisu-za in 1885.

1901 Lillie Langtry appears as Marie Antoinette in *A Royal Necklace* at the Imperial Theatre, London.

1913 Danish sculptor Edvard Eriksen completes the bronze 'The Little Mermaid' in Copenhagen.

1937 Britain's first Motor Show takes place at Olympia, London.

1900~1950

Back to Basics

Shakespeare enters the 20th century

If the popularity of Shakespeare's work increased during the 19th century, it blossomed in the early 20th. And this enthusiasm was travelling further, too. From the time of the 'Sturm und Drang' movement of the late 18th century, the German people have loved the Bard's plays, probably more than any other European nation (even calling him 'our Shakespeare' – cheek!). Notable performances included Max Reinhardt's productions at the New Theatre (1904), Bertolt Brecht's Coriolanus, *and the productions of Rudolf Schaller.*

A ll over the West ridiculously opulent Victorian sets and costumes were in decline owing to escalating costs. The English designer Edward Gordon Craig, however, remained something of an exception. A joint production of *Hamlet* with Constantin Stanislavsky at the Moscow Arts Theatre in 1912 resulted in Craig's elaborate designs falling down on opening night!

In the US, Shakespeare also became a mainstay of the classical repertoire. Of the great American Shakespearean actors, *Robert MANTELL* (1857–1907) was perhaps the last of the old school, but others included *John BARRYMORE* (1882–1942), *Eva Le GALLIENNE* (1899–1991), *Orson WELLES* (1915–85), *Julia MARLOWE*

Ooooh, Matron!

For Romeo, his first ever Shakespearean role, John Gielgud describes how he looked every inch the dashing young heart-throb! In 'white tights with soles attached... my feet looked enormous. My wig was coal black... parted in the middle. Wearing orange make-up and a very low-necked doublet [I looked] a mixture of Rameses of Egypt and a Victorian matron.'

Who's in the fun fur and leather, then? Orson Welles (who else?) as Macbeth.

1946 The newly completed Flamingo Hotel in Las Vegas is the first hotel in the city to operate as a hotel-casino resort.

1947 The first commercial microwave oven is introduced by the Raytheon Co in the US.

1953 Samuel Beckett writes *Waiting for Godot*, featuring the long-suffering tramps Vladimir and Estragon.

(1866–1950), *Richard* MANSFIELD (1854–1907) and *Katherine* CORNELL (1893–1974). *Paul* ROBESON (1898–1976) made a superb Othello in 1943, with *Jose* FERRER (1912–92) as Iago.

In Britain, *Laurence* OLIVIER (1907–89), *Vivien* LEIGH (1913–67), *John* GIELGUD (1904–2000) and *Ralph* RICHARDSON (1902–83) stood apart from the rest for the sheer weight of their performance, with perhaps Olivier giving the more 'Elizabethan' interpretations in his flamboyance and vigour. Olivier also moved the Bard more firmly into film.

Shakespeare had first reached Japan in 1885, and more productions followed in the early 1900s, including *Macbeth*, *Othello* and *King Lear*. In 1928, Dr Tsubouchi made important translations of the plays, and in 1929, Ichikawa Sanki formed the Shakespeare Association of Japan.

But Shakespeare was now struggling against an enormous proliferation of new theatre, dramatic theories, acting styles and writing. Psychology, too, helped

> ### DRAMATIS PERSONAE
>
> During Gielgud's 1934 production of Hamlet, with Gielgud himself in the title role, an army major visited Frank Vosper (playing Claudius) during the interval to congratulate him on his performance. This clearly went to his head, for, as Gielgud recounted, in the final scene, instead of saying 'Cousin Hamlet, you know the wager', Claudius demanded sonorously; 'Cousin Hamlet, you know the major!' Now, that's what you call a Major Slipup!

stimulate the changing attitudes to acting and theatre 'realism'. In Russia, Stanislavsky was urging the world of theatre forward with his actor training, in which the inner motivations of the *actor* were paramount to good characterization. Following his writings, the Method School flourished in America, which centred on an extreme naturalism where the actor *becomes* the character, thus denying the broader strokes of conventional character portrayal.

Robeson playing Othello (above), while Olivier (Romeo) canoodles with Vivien Leigh (Juliet), right.

GROUNDLINGS' GOSSIP

In 1937, Olivier's production of *Macbeth* seemed doomed. Olivier himself narrowly missed death when a weight crashed to the stage from the flies. Then a car accident nearly killed the director and Lady Macduff. Finally the theatre's proprietor died of a heart attack during the dress rehearsal.

1950 'You will find love the day you can show your weakness without the other person using it to affirm his strength', writes Cesare Pavese shortly before he commits suicide.

1952 Avant-garde composer John Cage performs his first 'Happening' in the US.

1956 The newly formed English Stage Company performs John Osborne's revolutionary *Look Back in Anger.*

1950~the present
Global Billing!
Adaptations, trapezes and rod puppets

Since the Second World War, Shakespeare's work has enjoyed revivals, adaptations, re-stagings, up-dating and just about any and all appropriations imaginable, all over the world. As the new media and communications networks have multiplied and spread their tentacles throughout the world, so his words have reached and influenced an ever-widening audience.

The spare setting of Peter Brook's *A Midsummer Night's Dream* (1970).

MacToast
An open-air production of *Macbeth* in Bermuda, starring Charlton Heston, hit on a great idea in having the soldiers burn Macbeth's castle to the ground. Unfortunately, the opening night was windy and flames and smoke were blown over the audience, who ran for their lives.

While the Royal Shakespeare Company has kept the flag flying in England, many other countries hold festivals celebrating his work, and most of his plays have been put in the school curriculum (too often accompanied by youthful groans and yawning). Landmark productions have been numerous, but Peter Hall's *A Midsummer Night's Dream* at Stratford, 1963, and Peter Brook's version of 1970, with everyone flying about on trapezes, stand out, as does

French farce
Shakespeare wasn't so popular everywhere. In France he'd never been accepted as readily as elsewhere, mainly because he wasn't French (and they did have Molière after all). In 1914 Georges Pellissier wrote, 'Let us have the courage...to say "The God of the Theatre" is a very bad dramatist' (making Britain's entry into a European Federal State look increasingly unlikely) although he did submit that Shakespeare could be called a 'great poet'. How generous.

Olivier's *Hamlet* (1963) starring Peter O'Toole. In the US, Shakespeare's work is kept alive in the universities, and at the many festivals held there, such as that at the American Shakespeare Theater at Stratford, Connecticut.

By 1961 Penguin publishers had sold over 2.5 million copies of Shakespeare's *Four Great Tragedies* in the US alone. In Russia Shakespeare's works have always been popular, and after the 1917 Revolution his words held new significance. Lunacharsky, the People's Commissar of Enlightenment (no, it was a *real* job!) had urged that

1972 US television premieres the comedy/drama series 'M*A*S*H'.

1976 The Apple computer company is founded in a California garage by college dropouts Stephen G. Wozniak and Steven Jobs.

1989 Architect I.M. Pei completes Hong Kong's 70-storey Bank of China Building, the tallest structure in the crown colony.

Shakespeare, like Schiller, must be 'resurrected'. *Coriolanus* was seen as particularly relevant to the class struggle. The Bard's writings are even more popular in Russia today.

In India it was natural that the colonial masters should take their Shakespeare with them. As British rule ended, India developed her own versions of the plays, such as *Behari-Talwar* ('Double-edged Sword'), a rendering of *Macbeth*. A production of *A Midsummer Night's Dream* set in Shimla at the turn of the century made Theseus a British colonist, had a group of Indian tradesmen playing the 'rude mechanicals', cast Hindu gods Rama and Sita as

acbeth ocated to e East, by anghai njr.

'This paint's set hard! I can't move my lips!' Keitoku Takata as a very scary Lear at the Tokyo Globe in 1991.

GROUNDLINGS' GOSSIP

Italians have always had their own take on Shakespeare. Early 20th-century productions of *Othello* had audiences screaming for Othello to give Iago what was coming to him. In 1948 a production of *As You Like It*, called *Rosalinda*, featured costumes by Salvador Dali, complete with antlers fixed onto the cod-pieces ('Are those antlers you're wearing, or are you just pleased to see me?').

Oberon and Titania, and replaced the fairies with Indian rod puppets. In recent years the plays have been translated into all the major dialects. In South Africa, the Shakespeare Society was formed in 1984 at the National Arts Festival in Grahamstown. And in Japan, Tadashi Suzuki has produced versions of *King Lear* and *Macbeth* using Japanese acting styles.

1901 In Britain, James Gibb invents the game of ping-pong.

1935 Stevens builds the first electronic hearing aid. It weighs just over 1 kg (2 lb).

1938 Nestlé markets instant coffee.

1899~2000
All the World's a Sound Stage
Shakespeare in 2-D

Orson Welles as Othello in his 1952 film. Suzanne Clautier plays Desdemona.

There have been several hundred films and television recordings of Shakespeare's plays made throughout the world since Sir Herbert Beerbohm Tree produced his triumphant stare-and-grimace silent classic, King John, *in 1899. From such two-reelers to glossy, star-studded Hollywood and Bollywood mega-productions, the Bard has had his poetry and ideas interpreted, re-interpreted and sometimes completely re-written so often that he must be turning in his grave like a chicken on a spit. There have been updates, backdates, gender-benders and cartoons, in all genres and his best and most famous plays have provided plots for a host of entertainments from the sublime to the spectacularly dreadful and embarrassingly inane.*

Traditionally, it has been the Old Boy's *words* that set the yardstick for quality – during the 19th century the idea was born that only a *literary* interpretation of Shakespeare's works was the true, natural and eternal one. This meant that the wonderful early silent film versions of the works weren't taken seriously by the

A star is born
Predictably, *Hamlet* has inspired more films than any other Shakespeare play. There have been at least 45 versions of either the whole play or parts of it, and at least 90 others that allude to it in some way. Most of these films have been British or American, but some are from places as diverse as India, Poland, Brazil and Japan.

1958 In Britain, the Queen's Christmas speech is televised for the first time.

1959 The first motorway (the M1) opens in Britain.

1975 NBC's *Saturday Night Live* is shown on American television with Chevy Chase, John Belushi, Gilda Radner, Bill Murray and Dan Aykroyd.

academy, who termed them 'dumb shows' because they relied on gesture and facial expression. But following the advent of sound critics must have breathed a sigh of relief, because once again they could elevate the 'literary'.

In television, the 1937 production of *Much Ado About Nothing* was the first to be seen in the UK, and in the US it was the

A futuristic Prospero and Miranda on the Forbidden Planet, one of many Bardic sci-fi reincarnations.

GROUNDLINGS' GOSSIP

Many films and television programmes have made liberal use of Shakespearean ideas and plots. Among the best known are *Forbidden Planet* (1956) which is a version of *The Tempest*, and many of the *Star Trek* plots *(see page 132)*. If the Bard himself could have witnessed such ingenuity, he might have quoted Hamlet: 'What a piece of work is man! How noble in reason!'

1953 *King Lear*, directed by Peter Brook and starring Orson Welles. Since then there has been a spate of popular films about Shakespeare's work or life that have emphasized the visual, and have either re-interpreted his work and its character relationships, or otherwise tried to bring him up to date with end-of-the-century developments in art: Franco Zeffirelli's sexy *Romeo and Juliet* (1968), Polanski's gory and creepy *Macbeth* (1971), more recently *Shakespeare In Love* (John Madden, 1999), *10 Things I Hate About You* (Gil Junger, 1999) based on *The Taming of the Shrew* (and surely one of the worst film titles ever), *Romeo and Juliet* (Baz Luhrmann, 1996) and *Much Ado About Nothing* (Kenneth Branagh, 1993). Films from non-English-speaking traditions are also highly interesting, as they have relocated and reappraised the text to fit their own culture *(see page 106)*.

Leo DiCaprio (Romeo) goes walkabout during filming and gets horribly lost on the set of a Madonna video.

1899 Ernest Rutherford, New Zealand physicist, discovers alpha and beta rays.

1913 Charlie Chaplin is discovered in New York and signs a $150-a-week contract to make movies.

1920 Soluble catgut is used to stitch up wounds for the first time.

1899~the present

Shakespeare Recharged and Reborn
The Bard in British films and television

A Hamlet rendered speechless.

It would seem that nearly as many Shakespeare films were produced in the UK and US before 1915 as have been made since then. Before the First World War, his work constituted a film genre on its own with its own set of production values for an identifiable, vast and very appreciative audience. There was a much closer relationship between theatre and film than there is now, and these first silent films, including the 1911 Macbeth *with Frank Benson in the title role, Benson's own* Richard III *of 1911 and Johnstone Forbes-Robertson's 1913* Hamlet, *were very theatrical in delivery.*

In some ways, the productions by Laurence Olivier of *Henry V* (1944), *Hamlet* (1948) and *Richard III* (1955) still reflected the Victorian Shakespearean tradition in England. Since the turn of the century, theatre and film had changed radically in Europe and North America. Only Britain, resistant as ever to new ideas, maintained a traditional and uniquely English production style, which was thought of as culturally superior. Elsewhere, the theatre work of artists such as Edward Gordon Craig, the Swiss Adolphe Appia and the French film pioneer George Méliès were influencing film-making with their ideas about using *light* to define mood, and spatial environment.

Other highlights of Shakespearean efforts on screen are *The Tower of London*, an interesting 1939 B-movie version of *Richard III*, starring

> **Moor stains**
> One story has it that during Stuart Burge's 1965 film of *Othello*, Laurence Olivier, all blacked up nicely for the part of the Moor, found that his make-up rubbed off on Desdemona (Maggie Smith) during the final scenes. Must have used the cheap stuff, or else he was just pressing against her *very hard*.

The Tower of London, with Boris Karloff and Basil Rathbone (1939).

1939 Pianist Myra Hess holds the first lunchtime concert in London's National Gallery, as a symbol of cultural resistance to the evening blackouts.

1960 Tokyo's Stationery Co introduces the Pentel, the world's first felt-tip pen.

1980 A fire at the 7-year-old MGM Grand Hotel in Las Vegas traps 3,500 guests, killing 84 people. Helicopters rescue more than 1,000 by lifting them from the roof.

Munchkins in Derek Jarman's version of *The Tempest* of 1979.

the 1930s, with Ian McKellen as Richard; Derek Jarman's beautiful *The Tempest* (1979); and, best known of all, *Shakespeare in Love* (1999). Kenneth Branagh's *Love's Labour's Lost* (2000) is one of

Basil Rathbone as Richard and with Boris Karloff in a role invented for the film; John Gielgud's 1964 *Hamlet*, with Richard Burton as Hamlet; Kenneth Branagh's *Henry V* (1989) and *Hamlet* (1996) with himself in the title roles. There has been a revival of interest in Shakespeare in the movies in recent years, and several inventive productions have emerged, such as Peter Greenaway's *Prospero's Books* (1991), with Gielgud as Prospero; Richard Moncraine's *Richard III*, an Anglo-American production set in a mythical fascist London of

the latest. However, from the 1960s Shakespeare was more frequently seen on British television. Some notable productions include Laurence Olivier as Shylock in Jonathan Miller's *The Merchant of Venice* (1973) and Olivier again as Lear in Michael Elliott's adaptation (1984).

Ian McKellen looking shifty as Richard Moncraine's fascist Richard III.

GROUNDLINGS' GOSSIP

Peter Brook's film of *King Lear* (1971), starring great actors such as Paul Scofield, Cyril Cusack and Jack MacGowan, upset many critics. They complained that it was too slow, while still promoting a 'high class theatre experience intended for a sensitive audience'. Brook has since largely confined himself to live theatre.

DRAMATIS PERSONAE

Honourable Murder (1960), a version of *Julius Caesar* scripted by Brian Clemens,

included in the cast one Philip Saville as Mark Antony. Saville went on to direct some wonderful British television programmes such as the original *Boys from the Blackstuff* (1980), *The Lives and Loves of a She-Devil* (1990) and *Metroland* (1997).

1913 Cecil B. DeMille's *The Squaw Man* becomes the first full-length feature to be filmed in Hollywood.

1929 Dunlop develops foam rubber for use as a padding material.

1954 American artist Jasper Johns paints his first 'Flag' painting, marking the emergence of Pop Art.

1900~the present

Shakespeare Rewritten and Repackaged
US films and the Great Welles

Vitagraph's Macbeth *in 1908 sparked off a growth in Shakespearean films in the US just as Tree's* King John *had done in the UK. During the following 12 months, Vitagraph went on to produce six more Shakespeare plays, including* Romeo and Juliet, Othello *and* The Merchant of Venice. *In 1908 the omnipresent D.W. Griffiths waded in with* The Taming of the Shrew.

Pickford and Fairbanks (top); Mickey Rooney as Puck (above).

Revenge is sweet
In playing *Richard III*, Olivier apparently staged his own revenge drama. As he recounted, 'Nose on, wig on, makeup complete. There, staring back at me from the mirror, was my Richard…I'd based the makeup on the American theatre director Jed Harris, the most loathsome man I'd ever met. My revenge on Harris was complete.'

In 1929, Sam Taylor produced the silent *The Taming of the Shrew* with Mary Pickford and Douglas Fairbanks. It was famous for its writing credits: 'Written by William Shakespeare with Additional Dialogue by Sam Taylor'. It was supposedly based on David Garrick's performing edition of the play, though heavily cut and done in the style of silent pantomime and declamatory theatre. In 1935 Warner Brothers released the Max Reinhardt and William Dieterle version of *A Midsummer Night's Dream*. All Warner's top stars were cast, including James Cagney as Bottom, and Mickey Rooney as Puck, and choreography was done by Nijinsky. Reinhardt was employing theories lifted from Appia, which he had earlier tried out in a production of the play at the Hollywood Bowl

River Phoenix and Keanu Reeves in *Henry IV, Part One* updated.

A FILM BY GUS VAN SANT

my own private IDAHO RIVER PHOENIX KEANU

whatever it takes to have a r

1964 James Earl Jones plays the title role in a New York production of *Othello*.

1973 The video recorder enters the home for the first time; 30 years later, people will still have trouble pre-setting them.

1999 Latin fever hits the pop scene as Latin-influenced music by the likes of Ricky Martin, Julio Iglesias, Marc Anthony and even ex-Spice girl Geri Halliwell floods the charts.

in 1934. When Laurence Olivier's 1955 movie of *Richard III* debuted on NBC television it was watched by some 50 million people, more than had seen the play in its entire production history!

Al Pacino looking in a mirror and finding Richard.

Other great productions of Shakespeare on the American screen are the *Tragedy of Othello: The Moor of Venice*, directed by Orson Welles (1952), and funded by the US, Italy, France and Morocco, with Welles as Othello and Micheál MacLiammóir as Iago (held by many to be one of the very finest Shakespeare films, with its excellent use of black-and-white cinematography emphasizing architecture as emotional environment), and Al Pacino's *Looking For Richard* (1996), with Pacino as Richard III and everyone who was anyone tagging along. *My Own Private Idaho* (Gus Van Sant, 1992) was a version of *Henry IV Part One* and *Bugsy* (Barry Levinson, 1991) took its plot from *Antony and Cleopatra*. Actors who have played Othello include Raul Julia

DRAMATIS PERSONAE

John Cassavetes and Gena Rowlands, two of cinema's finest acting marriage partners, starred in Paul Mazursky's The Tempest *(1982), alongside Susan Sarandon. Mazursky was influenced by Che Xuan's* General Tsao Lightning *(1966). Oh yes, and Raul Julia plays a goatherd who owns a Sony Trinitron and lives in a cave.*

in Joseph Papp's 1979 version, Yaphet Kotto (1980) and Laurence Fishburne (1995). Tony Curtis had a challenging role to play as General Iago in Max Boulois' *Othello, The Black Commando*, a film that was produced jointly in France and Spain in 1982.

Laurence Fishburne looking like he's ready to strangle someone.

1900 Grand Duke Constantine of Russia, uncle of the Czar, translates *Hamlet* into Russian, and plays the title role in a performance at the Winter Palace, St Petersburg.

1930 Architect Le Corbusier completes Maison Savoye at Poissy-sur-Seine, France.

1936 In Paris the first speaking clock comes into service.

1900~the present

Spaghetti Westerns and Cartoons
Shakespeare films in Europe

Sarah Bernhardt as Hamlet, about to make a point

After Sir Herbert Beerbohm Tree's 1899 film of King John, Clement Maurice *filmed* Hamlet *(1900) in France with Sarah Bernhardt as Hamlet. Georges Méliès made a version of* Hamlet *in 1907. The same year, in Germany, Franz Porten and his wife filmed* Othello, *and in Italy, Mario and Maria Caserini produced* Otello. *It was so successful that the pair went on to do* Romeo and Juliet *together the next year (what is it with these husband and wife acts?). The following year it was France's turn again with* Le Songe d'une nuit d'été. *And so it went on all over Europe, production after production.*

But as in America and Britain, European films of Shakespeare's plays shrank somewhat by the 1960s. Television showed more interest, especially in England and

> **GROUNDLINGS' GOSSIP**
>
> **I**n Italy, a spaghetti western version of *Hamlet*, *Quella sporca storia nel west*, also known as *Johnny Hamlet*, or *That Dirty Story of the West*, came out in 1968. It was directed by Enzo Castellari, who the year before had made *Vado... l'ammazzo e torno (For a Few Bullets More).*

Scandinavia, as did radio, and at the same time the plays became essential reading for most Western educational systems. In the early 1990s a series of Russian animated films entitled *Shakespeare: Animated Tales* was made for television as well as for the growing video market, and shown in Britain on the BBC. They included most of Shakespeare's main tragedies and comedies, and were mostly cut down to run approximately 30 minutes. As an enterprise targeting a young audience, they have been very successful, selling to television companies

1955 Artificial diamonds are produced.

1995 *Toy Story*, the first film to be made entirely with computer-animated characters, is released in the US.

2000 A total lunar eclipse occurs at the time of the full moon for the the first time in 133 years. The moon appears 33 per cent larger and brighter than normal.

A Dutch poster for *A Midsummer Night's Dream*. Nice teeth, shame about the ears!

in at least 30 countries. Whether they will ever make any difference to the classroom gloom that most teachers manage to spread when 'teaching' Shakespeare is another matter altogether.

Despite smaller audiences, filmed versions continued throughout the century, though what was done to them sometimes just to gain the attention of an audience is nobody's business. Finland banned the 1968 US production of soft-porn movie *The Secret Sex Lives of Romeo and Juliet*

(although they did produce a rather bizarre black-and-white version of Hamlet called *Hamlet liikemaailmassa* – or *Hamlet Gets Business* – in 1987). More serious European films included *Dvenadtsataya noch*, a Russian *Twelfth Night* (1992), scripted by Leon Garfield, whereas television productions included *Komediya oshibok (The Comedy of Errors)* in Russia in 1978, and *Der Kaufmann von Venedig (The Merchant of Venice)* in Germany (1990). Of course, we mustn't forget Franco Zeffirelli's Anglo/European comic-book production of *Hamlet* (1990) starring a dashing Mel Gibson as the Dane.

The handsome prince at rest. Mel Gibson in Franco Zeffirelli's film.

The Bardfather
One of the strangest versions of *King Lear* was by cult French director Jean-Luc Godard in 1987. It was co-written by Norman Mailer and starred Woody Allen (as Mr Alien), Peter Sellers (as Shakespeare), Norman and Kate Mailer (as themselves) and Burgess Meredith as mobster Don Learo! Godard is also in it as a professor who keeps on photocopying his hand.

1913 In Moscow playwright-poet Vladimir Vladimirovich Mayakovsky performs in his own play *Vladimir Mayakovsky – A Tragedy.*

1931 New Delhi, the planned capital designed by British architects Edwin Landseer Lutyens and Herbert Baker and inspired by Christopher Wren and Pierre L'Enfant, is completed in India.

1950 The Mambo is introduced from Cuba to New York dance floors.

1900~the present
From Bombay to Mexico
A truly universal Bard

During the 20th century, as the technology rapidly spread from the West, film became just as big an attraction worldwide. And the plays of Shakespeare, although nowhere near as popular as in the West, still jumped from stage to screen. But the cultural differences are great, so it has been Shakespeare's central stories that have held interest, not the 'English' customs, costumes, sets or language that, to us, seem so much an intrinsic part. China, Japan, India etc. all had their own ancient theatre forms doing very nicely, thank you very much, without an imported 'Bard'; and translation wasn't easy, to say the least.

The great director Akira Kurosawa's *Throne of Blood.*

In Japan, the most famous film director, and one of the best in the world, is Akira Kurosawa. In 1957 Kurosawa made a version of *Macbeth*, called *Kumonosujo* ('Throne of Blood'), which, in 1965, was described as the only film ever to succeed in 'transforming a play of Shakespeare's into film'. It leans towards expressionism, in that, for example, it uses the forest as a visual expression of Macbeth's mind. In 1985 he made another Shakespearean film, *Ran*, based on *King Lear*, which, despite its undeniable brilliance, was criticized in the West because Kurosawa had the nerve to change the daughters to sons.

Kurosawa's *Ran.* His film adaptations give scale and grandeur to the plays.

1965 Dolby noise reduction equipment becomes available.

1974 *People* magazine begins publication in New York City.

1993 Stephen Spielberg's dinosaur fantasy *Jurassic Park* becomes the highest-ever box-office grossing film.

(In traditional Japanese culture daughters would never inherit a kingdom from their father, so something had to give.)

In India a huge film industry sprang up during the century, centred on Bombay. As early as 1935, Sohrab Modi made a version of *Hamlet* called *Khoon Ka Khoon*, followed in 1948 by Akhtar Hussein's *Anjuman (Romeo and Juliet)*; six years later Kishore Sahu produced *Hamlet*. In 1997, Jayaraaj Rajasekharan Nair made *Kaliyattam (Othello)*, also known as *Play*

Asta Nielsen's gender-bending Hamlet

demonstrating Scandinavian angst gesture No. 1.

of the God using traditional characters in place of Shakespeare's. In other countries, productions have been much thinner, with only a few notable exceptions that should be mentioned here. In Egypt a localized version of *Romeo And Juliet*, titled *Shuhaddaa el gharam*, was made in 1942 by Kamal Selim, and *The Taming of The Shrew*, as *Cartas marcadas*, was made in Mexico, in 1948, by René Cardona.

GROUNDLINGS' GOSSIP

Asta Nielsen's 1921 *Hamlet* was, er, interesting. German-made, but with a Danish lead actor and director, it apparently contained a few useful additions from a 12th-century Danish historian. It was also noteworthy for explaining that Hamlet behaved as he did because 'he' was a 'she'!

Sergei Bondarchuk gives Desdemona one final flash of his dark and brooding eyes.

Red Russian

Sergei Yutkevich's Russian film of *Othello* of 1955 contained some great moments of high camp. Sergei Bondarchuk, playing Othello, was caught in fishing nets to illustrate how he was mentally ensnared (subtle!), and his eyes flashed red when he was angry! By all accounts he made a 'mild, rather stupid, Othello, so that one's interest…[lay] with the devilish Iago'.

107

1835 Marie Grosholtz moves her waxwork collection to Baker Street, London, and opens the permanent home for 'Madame Tussaud's'.

1839 The Anglo-Chinese opium war is fought.

1850 *Harper's Monthly* is published for the first time in New York.

1827~the present

Was there Life before the RSC?
From festival to institution and beyond

Stratford celebrates its famous son.

The Royal Shakespeare Company, formed in 1961, was not the first attempt at a Stratford theatre devoted to the works of Shakespeare. The town had long held ambitions to keep itself firmly on the Shakespearean map (see also page 22). However, it was a long journey from rather ad hoc summer festivals to the stable company that has thrilled audiences for the last 30 years.

In 1769 Stratford held a Jubilee, featuring David Garrick. It wasn't a great success, but Stratford Council continued the tradition until 1824, when the Shakespearean Club was formed at the Falcon Inn. Three years later a three-day festival was held; 40,000 visitors attended, and a cornerstone was laid at New Place for a theatre (not Stratford's first, but

Garrick nodding off in the Green Room.

the biggest), and the good Burghers of Stratford resolved to hold such a bash every three years. Just to confuse everyone, the True Blue Shakespeare Club then formed, announcing that it too would have a three-year festival. The Shakespearean Club fought back with patronage from George IV, and changed its name to the Royal Shakespearean Club. The theatre, whose cornerstone was laid in 1827, was first called the Shakespearean Theatre, then the Royal Shakespearean Theatre and finally the Theatre Royal. But it wasn't a success and was torn down in 1872 by its owner, who preferred a garden. The first Shakespeare Memorial Theatre opened in Stratford in 1879, with, appropriately, *Much Ado About Nothing*.

> **GROUNDLINGS' GOSSIP**
>
> In February 2000 the RSC began its world tour of *The Taming of the Shrew*. Five articulated trucks transported over 43 tonnes of equipment – everything needed to create a high-tech mobile theatre auditorium for performances in school halls and leisure centres.

1884 A line through the Greenwich Observatory, London, becomes the zero line of longitude and local time is known as Greenwich Mean Time.

1890 Ivanovsky discovers the first viruses while studying diseases found in tobacco plants.

1950 The board game 'Scrabble' is invented.

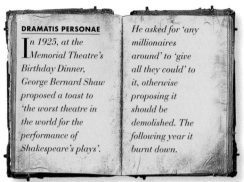

DRAMATIS PERSONAE

In 1925, at the Memorial Theatre's Birthday Dinner, George Bernard Shaw proposed a toast to 'the worst theatre in the world for the performance of Shakespeare's plays'. He asked for 'any millionaires around' to 'give all they could' to it, otherwise proposing it should be demolished. The following year it burnt down.

The Shakespeare Memorial Theatre was destroyed by fire in 1926 and in 1932 a new theatre was commissioned, and paid for with money from benefactors from England, America, Canada and, of course, from the King. This theatre (called by some 'a tomb' or 'a jam factory' – although old Bernard Shaw liked it) flourished under Anthony Quayle, and Glen Byam Shaw. When Peter Hall became director in 1958, the Royal Shakespeare Company was formed. A second space, The Other Place, was opened in Stratford, and the Aldwych in London took on duties as yet another connected venue. These days the Barbican has that honour.

Since 1978 the Royal Shakespeare Company also tours, not only in Great Britain but also throughout the world, and runs educational courses and other events to stay solvent (it receives vast sums of public money as well). In 1999, its production of *Richard III* took over £1 million. The same year its Summer Festival Season of a ten-play repertoire had sold over £2 million worth of tickets before the opening night of the first production in March.

Bard's bonus
Admiration for the RSC has spread throughout the world. For example, its Head of Music, Stephen Warbeck, received an Oscar nomination for his soundtrack for the much-acclaimed film *Shakespeare in Love*, which featured actors from the company.

The cast of *Shakespeare in Love* are told of the box office receipts.

1970 A 60,000–100,000-tonne oil spillage called 'the Othello' occurs after a collision in Tralhavet Bay, Sweden.

1976 In Britain, workmen discover a perfectly preserved rose that had been cemented into a wall in Romsey Abbey in 1120.

1982 MRI (Magnetic Resonance Imaging) machines are introduced in Britain providing the medical service with a superior form of scanning tool to the CAT scan.

1968~2000

Globes around the Globe
The Bankside dream and a Texas timewarp

For the existence of the new London Globe theatre on Bankside we can thank a somewhat irritated actor from Chicago. Sam Wanamaker CBE first came to Britain in 1949 to star in the film Give Us This Day. *Because he loved Shakespeare and had started his acting career playing him at the Great Lakes World Fair in Cleveland, Ohio, he wanted to see the site of the original theatre. But to his astonishment and irritation, all he found was a small plaque on a brewery wall.*

Sam with a model of his dream.

An elemental performance
The London Globe is open-air, audiences come and go as they please, there are short pauses instead of artificial intervals, actors and audiences are close, and everyone has fun. The 'groundlings' stand in the yard getting wet if it rains, or roasted if it's hot, and the 'rich' sit under cover – but also get burned sometimes. Just how it should be!

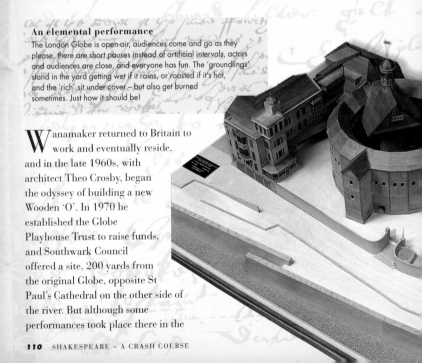

Wanamaker returned to Britain to work and eventually reside, and in the late 1960s, with architect Theo Crosby, began the odyssey of building a new Wooden 'O'. In 1970 he established the Globe Playhouse Trust to raise funds, and Southwark Council offered a site, 200 yards from the original Globe, opposite St Paul's Cathedral on the other side of the river. But although some performances took place there in the

1984 The Dallas Museum of Art, a giant limestone building designed by Edward Larrabee Barnes, opens, replacing the 81-year-old Museum of Fine Arts.

1985 Japanese director Kurosawa releases his film *Ran*, a reworking of *King Lear*.

1996 In the US, a domestic cat chokes on his flea collar and manages to hit speed dial and reach 911 (emergency services). Police locate the cat and remove the collar.

1970s, under canvas, foundations for the new theatre were not dug until 1989. The Bremer Shakespeare Company performed *The Merry Wives of Windsor* in the partially built theatre in 1993. Sadly, a few months later, Sam Wanamaker died, before his 25-year dream was fully realized. A year later, Theo Crosby also died. In 1997 the Globe was formally opened and is now the pride of London – thanks to a great and determined Uncle Sam.

America has always regarded Shakespeare with affection, but nowhere quite so much as Odessa in Texas, which took it upon itself during the 1960s to build and run a replica of the original Elizabethan Globe. This 410-seat octagonal theatre was the brainchild of a local teacher, Marjorie Wallace. Wallace

Henry V is played at the new Globe theatre to a full house.

gained support from internationally acclaimed scholar Allardyce Nicoll, who said, 'If you complete this theatre…you will have the most nearly authentic replica of Shakespeare's own Globe anywhere on earth'. This 'Globe' produces the Bard's works alongside Gilbert and Sullivan and monthly country-and-western shows called 'The Brand New Opree'. A replica of Anne Hathaway's Cottage was also added in 1988. Other theatres have taken the name only, such as the American Globe Theater in New York, and the Old Globe Theater in San Diego, California.

A model of the reconstruction of Shakespeare's Globe.

GROUNDLINGS' GOSSIP

Sam Wanamaker didn't just give us a new Globe. He produced, directed and starred in Clifford Odets' *Winter Journey* with Sir Michael Redgrave; he took over Liverpool's Shakespeare Theatre, creating the first arts and performance centre in Britain; he played Iago in the Royal Shakespeare Theatre's *Othello*; and he perfected many other film and theatre roles as well.

1775 Bath's Royal Crescent is completed by English architect John Wood the Younger.

1838 In Khiva, Russia, a British colonel, accused of failing to show the emir proper respect, is thrown into a pit of flesh-eating vermin.

1876 The Glacerium, the first ice rink, opens in London.

1769~the present

A Whole Lotta Shakespeare Goin' On!
Shakespeare festivals around the world

Following the lead of those 18th-century Shakespeare festivals in Stratford, many others have sprung up around the world especially in China, Japan, New Zealand, South Africa and some European countries. There are over 100 Shakespeare festivals in the US and Canada alone, one of the oldest being the Ashland Shakespeare Festival, in Ashland, Oregon; the largest is the Alabama Shakespeare Festival, in Montgomery, Alabama. In Canada there's the Stratford, Ontario, festival, while in Tokyo there's a Shakespeare theme park with a full-size reproduction of Shakespeare's home-town.

Sets by Richard L. Hay made *Two Gentlemen of Verona* at Ashland, Oregon in 1974 more memorable than most.

Of the Australian festivals, the Shakespeare Festival Australia had a bash after the 2000 Olympic Games in Sydney, and in Southern Highlands NSW, a cultural tourism project is under way to build a replica Elizabethan playhouse based on Inigo Jones' 1600 design to convert the Royal Cockpit-in-Court gaming house to a permanent theatre. This project, which also features a museum, will be a platform for Australian contributors to the works of William Shakespeare. The integral museum will have a 'Replica Elizabethan Playhouse; a time-line viewing area of Elizabethan life; a tire house set as it could have been in Shakespeare's day; Elizabethan stage effects, makeup, costume and sound effect equipment; Elizabethan musical

Alabama Bard
The $21.5 million Alabama Festival Theater was hailed as 'Brash and Brilliant' by the *New York Times*. The fifth largest Shakespeare festival in the world, it gets more than 300,000 visitors a year. It houses two theatres, production shops and rehearsal halls. And there is a John Quincy Adams Ward statue of William Shakespeare that proudly surveys the Grand Lobby.

1911 French mystery writer Gaston Leroux pens *The Phantom of the Opera*.

1913 The first US crossword puzzle appears in the weekend supplement of *New York World*.

1960 In Britain, Aldeburgh's Jubilee Hall stages the first production of the opera *A Midsummer Night's Dream* with music by Benjamin Britten and libretto from Shakespeare's comedy.

instruments and music for theatre, and a review and research area'. In South Australia, the Adelaide Festival for 2000 boasted a programme called 'Shakespeare Under the Stars; Text by William Shakespeare', drawing from pop music, rock imagery, pantomime and sitcom.

In the year 2000, 436 years after he was born, I think William Shakespeare would have been pretty pleased. South Africa's Standard Bank National Arts Festival included *Antony and Cleopatra*.

Promotional poster for a production of *Henry V* in Central Park.

Italy's Taormina Arte Festival had *Othello*. The Paris Autumn Festival had *Hamlet, Measure For Measure*, and the *Dream*, and the Avignon Festival featured *La Tempesta, Henri IV* and *Richard III*. At the International Festival of Classical Theatre in Almagro, Spain, *Jules Caesar* and *Taming of the Shrew* topped the bill, while the Barcelona Summer Festival Grec competed with *Hamlet* and *Macbeth*. In Hungary the regular Zsambeck Saturdays Festival features Shakespeare. In Turkey, the International Istanbul Theatre Festival offered *Romeo and Juliet* in a modern Turkish setting. Each year, everywhere, there's a whole lotta Shakespeare goin' on!

Showing today: *Hamlet*

Kronborg Castle at Elsinore, Denmark, has hosted the only festival dedicated entirely to productions of *Hamlet*. Inaugurated in 1937 by a performance given by Laurence Olivier and the Old Vic company, it has also seen performances by German director Gustav Gründgens in 1938, and John Gielgud in 1939. From 1954 there were no more performances until Derek Jacobi played *Hamlet* in 1978.

Hamlet's efforts to start a game of leapfrog go unnoticed.

1684 Croissants are baked in Vienna for the first time.

1740 The music for 'Rule Britannia' is composed.

1756 English civil engineer John Smeaton reintroduces the use of cement, for building the fourth Eddystone Lighthouse.

1590~the present

'Thou Wouldst Make a Good Fool'
Jig-dancing comedians and vaudevillians

Richard Tarleton.

'To be a comedian means in actuality to be an actor' observed *Max Wall, one of the greatest English clowns of the 20th century. Clowns have been as integral a part of Shakespeare's dramas as any tragic heroes or heroines. They have probably existed from the time people first laughed, but in Shakespeare's lifetime the most influential would have been the 'fools' in the local morality plays who were the only ones who dared to kick the devil's backside!*

Richard TARLETON (d. 1588), one of the Queen Elizabeth's Men, and probably the original source for Yorick in *Hamlet*, was the most famous of the Elizabethan clowns and inspirational to many of Shakespeare's plays. *William KEMPE* (d. 1603) succeeded him in the Queen Elizabeth's Men. He was notorious for adding bits of tomfoolery to the dialogue to delight his audiences, and it's thought *he* was the cause of Hamlet's advice to the players! Kempe played Launce and Speed (*The Two Gentlemen of Verona*), Bottom (*A Midsummer Night's Dream*) and Dogberry (*Much Ado About Nothing*) and there is little doubt his genius influenced

'Would you care to repeat that?'
Dogberry won't stand any Ado.

> **GROUNDLINGS' GOSSIP**
>
> American clowns Dan Rice and William R. Wallett travelled in mid-19th century circuses reciting pastiches of the Bard of Avon. As Wallett chanted 'Is this a dagger I see before me?', Rice interrupted with: 'Is that a beefsteak I see before me? With the burnt side toward my hand?'

1855 In Britain pub-goers riot against changes in Sunday openings hours.

1931 A Moscow hospital sets up a blood bank for the first time.

1957 The musical *West Side Story* opens at the Winter Garden Theater, New York. The story is based on Shakespeare's *Romeo and Juliet* with music by Leonard Bernstein and lyrics by Stephen Sondheim.

Shakespeare's writing. He was also a great improviser and, like Tarleton, a dancer, morris-dancing from London to Norwich.

From 1937, Jay Laurier, a music hall comedian, played many of Shakespeare's clowns at the Old Vic and at Stratford. *George ROBEY* (1869–1954) was the first, and perhaps the best, English music-hall clown to play Falstaff (*Henry IV*, 1935) at Her Majesty's Theatre. Critics reported that he was 'not only a genius, but [a] kindred genius of Shakespeare's own Falstaff', and that he was 're-Elizabethanizing' Shakespeare. Robey himself was so impressed with Shakespeare's 'gags' in the part that he 'wondered why

Thomas King as Touchstone in *As You Like It* (1767).

The English comic Sid James is one of many who have tackled the Bard.

Mobster Macbeth
English comedy actor Sid James, famous for his parts in the *Carry On* films, played Banky (Banquo) in the 1955 English film version of *Macbeth*, called *Joe MacBeth*. The story was Shakespeare in a gangster setting with Lily MacBeth persuading her husband Joe to kill the local crime boss (Duncan) and take over his patch.

he had spent a lifetime inventing his own'. In 1957, the English comedian *Frankie HOWERD* (1922–92) played Bottom at the Old Vic. One critic remarked that Howerd's performance proved 'that such parts come to life when a genuine clown [invests them with] his own personality'. The great American clown *Bert LAHR* (1895–1967) also played Bottom in the American Shakespeare Festival in 1960.

Not all clowns loved Shakespeare, though. Charlie Chaplin once said, 'I cannot pretend to enjoy Shakespeare…I feel I am listening to a scholarship oration'. Methinks he must have been going to see the wrong productions.

1592 A Russian census lists peasants under the names of landholders, as peasants are considered to be the landlords' serfs.

1594 Tintoretto dies and is buried in the church where his *Last Judgement* hangs.

1596 Tomatoes are introduced to England as ornamental plants.

1592~1611

A Pox on Thee!
Thou Bat-Fowling Puttock!
Shakespeare's insults

Shakespeare was not only a great poet, playwright, songwriter, creator of brilliant dialogue, characterization, plot and metaphor, etc., etc., he was also possibly the most accomplished inventor of insults the English language has ever thrown up!

A trade of insults with the noisy gang from *Twelfth Night*.

When it comes to subtle put-downs or just plain rudeness, Shakespeare is in a class of his own. It has been estimated that within his 38 plays are some 10,000 different insults. Shakespeare knew that the insult is a perfect way to demonstrate not only contempt but also erudition. Each play is full of them, from simple name-calling to very comprehensive character assassinations. A few names for your enemies: *'prating mountebank'*, *'whoreson dog'*, *'dunghill groom'*, *'tedious stumbling-block'*, *'swoll'n parcel of dropsies'* (one of my favourites). Prefer something more elaborate? How about *'anointed sovereign of sighs and groans'* or *'canker of a calm world and a long peace'*?

Here's a few for specific occasions. If you're about to divorce, remember, *'The first thing we do, let's kill all the lawyers'* (*Henry VI*). If a garrulous person annoys you, announce to all, *'This is a tale, told by an idiot, full of sound and fury, signifying nothing'* (*Macbeth*). The next time you are cornered by a bore at a party cry, *'If you be mad, be gone: if you have reason, be brief'* (*Twelfth Night*). Or if there's a gang of youths making a drunken racket outside your house at night, go out and say *'Have*

Tit for tat

Here's a couple for women to use: *'You poor inch of nature!'* (no prizes for guessing what that refers to); *'You whoreson beetle-headed, flap-ear'd knave'*; *'thou misshapen Dick'*! And for the men: *'You wanton calf, flax-wench, and callat of boundless tongue'*, *'leprous witch and stretched-mouthed rascal'*, *'hag of all despite'*!

1603 Walter Raleigh is tried for high treason, found guilty and imprisoned.

1608 In Chile a Spanish royal decree legalizes slavery of Chilean Indians.

1610 Henry IV of France is stabbed to death by a fanatical Catholic monk.

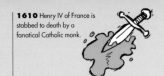

you no wit, manners, nor honesty, but to gabble like tinkers at this time of night?* (*Twelfth Night*) – on the other hand, perhaps that's not a such good idea.

Perhaps you wish to start a little salacious gossip about a neighbour? Then you could try saying that although he currently has his wife on his arm, he '*little thinks she has been sluic'd in's absence, And his pond fished by his next neighbour*' (*The Winter's Tale*)! If one of your employees misses an important meeting, say '*I will knog your urinal about your Knave's cogscomb for missing your meetings and appointments*' (*The Merry Wives of Windsor*). And for the next time your partner nags you, '*Thou hid'st a thousand daggers in thy thoughts, which thou hast whetted on thy stony heart, to stab at half an hour of my life*' (*Henry IV*).

'Beware, my Lord! She's a hag of all despite!' King Lear at the ENO, in 1989.

1594 In Germany, musician Orlando di Lasso, master of chapel music in Munich, dies. Known as 'Divino Orlando', he excelled in motets and songs.

1596 English playwright George Chapman's *The Blind Beggar of Alexandria* is performed at London's Rose theatre, by the Lord Admiral's Men.

1598 Henry IV of France issues 'The Edict of Nantes' allowing Protestants to worship according to their faith.

1592~1610
Those Words of Lurve
Mr Smooth gets in the Groove

Shakespeare knew how to express love and desire even better than disdain and loathing. His mind, constantly on the search for new ways to describe it, came up with 'word pictures' that portrayed not merely the conventional images, such as love as a furnace, *or a* fire, *or* lightning *or* thunder *(did the earth move for you too?), or even a* war *or a* state of siege *(now* there's *a familiar situation!), but also the nature of love by the depth of feelings and actions it provokes.*

'I think you're gorgeous! But my mum might not agree!'

Titania and Bottom canoodling in the *Dream*.

Mind you, Shakespeare wasn't above calling upon chubby little Cupid! 'You are a lover; borrow Cupid's wings, / And soar with them above a common bound' (*Romeo and Juliet*). Or how about: 'Love looks not with the eyes, but with the mind; / And therefore is winged Cupid painted blind' (*A Midsummer Night's Dream*). He also knew well the relationship between love, poetry and a certain madness that inflicts pain as it does pleasure. He might have been describing himself when he wrote: 'The lunatic, the lover, and the poet / Are of imagination all compact: / One sees more devils than vast hell can hold…, the lover… Sees Helen's beauty in a brow of Egypt: / The poet's… pen… turns them to shapes' (*A Midsummer Night's Dream*).

Love could be like food: 'So are you to my thoughts as food to life' (Sonnet 75). Or it is the envy of a common object because of its relationship to a loved one: 'See, how

1599 Poet Edmund Spenser dies; he is best remembered for his seven-volume poem 'The Faerie Queene', dedicated to Elizabeth I.

1600 In Barbados, the Spanish start producing a new spirit (rum) on sugar plantations.

1601 German authorities close many *Badestuben* (brothels) in an attempt to halt the spread of venereal disease.

Benedict and Beatrice discover they don't need too many words.

she leans her cheek upon her hand! / O that I were a glove upon that hand, / That I might touch that cheek!' (*Romeo and Juliet*). It could be a sickness, a raging fever, a breaking heart, an excess – either physically or metaphorically: *'If music be the food of love, play on; / Give me excess of it, that, surfeiting, the appetite may sicken, and so die'* (*Twelfth Night*). But it could also seem like a greedy child: *'That longs for everything that he can come by'*, and , *'like a testy babe, will scratch the nurse, And presently, all humbled, kiss the rod!'* (*Two Gentlemen of Verona*). A whole school of psychoanalytic thought (and the bread and butter of many a shrink) was born out of that last sentiment!

Moon swoon

And let's not forget that ol' Moon, which, whether it's in June or not, still hits the heart's lurve spot (see, I'm just as good as Shakespeare). *'O, swear not by the moon, the inconstant moon, / That monthly changes in her circled orb, / Lest that thy love prove likewise variable'* (*Romeo and Juliet*). Amen to that!

The trouble with too much moonlight: it brings out the giant flesh-eating moths.

GROUNDLINGS' GOSSIP

Shakespeare not only knew the difference between love and lust *(see page 79)*, he also thoroughly understood the wicked ways of men (I wonder why?): *'Sigh no more ladies, sigh no more / Men were deceivers ever / One foot in sea and one on shore, / To one thing constant never'* (*Much Ado About Nothing*).

1592 Morocco's Sultan Mulai Ahmed al-Mansur sends 4,000 Andalusian mercenaries and Christian renegades to invade Songhai with 8,000 camels and arms supplied by Elizabeth of England.

1595 The late Christopher Marlowe's *Dido, Queen of Carthage* is completed by Thomas Nashe.

1599 Sully creates the office of 'gran dvoyer' to begin the reform of the French road system.

1592~1610

'The Slime that Sticks on Filthy Deeds'

Spells, vile blackness and evil corruption

'Oh, save me, Hubert, save me!' (*King John*, Act IV).

The Elizabethan notion of evil was a scary one indeed. Still fuelled by medieval ideas of paganism, hellfire, retribution, grotesque characters such as the Green Man and the sacrificial killing of animals, terrible fears lurked in store for those who didn't live a morally healthy life. Even the Anglo-Saxon church used occultism as it took over pagan rites. Exorcism still occurred, not only to fight evil – 'Bell, book, and candle shall not drive me back, / When gold and silver becks me to come on' (King John) *– but also to make fields fertile, drive away rats and even to make rain!*

Burnt offerings
The Duke of Bedford, in *Henry VI*, says, 'Bonfires in France forthwith I am to make, / To keep our great Saint George's feast withal'. He is alluding to the burning of Joan of Arc later on. This was another all-too-common feature of the time: horrific and savage death for 'witchcraft', blasphemy or treason.

Shakespeare had access, then, to all sorts of images to describe and project evil, fear and sin. The colour black was a favourite: '*But if black scandal or foul-faced reproach*' (*Richard III*), '*Thou turn'st mine eyes into my very soul, / And there I see such black and grained spots*' (*Hamlet*). He puts this image to particular use in *Othello*, where, of course, the central character is black – a 'Moor'. Most uses of the word come from dastardly Iago: '*When devils will the blackest sins put on…So I will turn her virtue to pitch*' (fair makes you shudder don't it?). Later Othello, upon hearing about Desdemona's supposed

'Tighter! Tighter! Harder! Ooh yes, that's right!'

Richard III and Brakenbury up to a bit of S&M.

1600 In Rome, scientific monk and philosopher Giordano Bruno is burnt alive for his belief in an infinite universe with the sun at its centre.

1606 Flemish painter Peter Paul Rubens creates Genoa's 'Circumcision altarpiece'.

1610 In Jamestown, Virginia, during a winter of extreme hardship, a man is put to death for eating his wife's body.

Laurence Fishburne and Kenneth Branagh in *Othello*.

infidelity, laments, 'Her name, that was as fresh / As Dian's visage, is now begrimed and black / As mine own face'.

Evil is also a foul disease, an infection, a virus. The word 'corruption' was a favourite, and a very good word it is too. Shakespeare chose well when he had Lear call Goneril 'a boil, a plague-sore, an embossed carbuncle...in [my] corrupted blood' (*King Lear*) at a time when the plague was rife. All sins, like sicknesses, have a foul smell: 'Away with me, all you whose souls abhor, / The uncleanly savours of a slaughter-house; / For I am stifled with this smell of sin' (*King John*). John's own anger is described as a tumour, leaking 'foul corruption'. Antony, bemoaning the murder of Caesar, cries, '[it]..shall smell above the earth / With carrion men, groaning for burial' (*Julius Caesar*). And of course, there is the most famous of all quotes, 'Something is rotten in the state of Denmark' (*Hamlet*) which alludes to the smell of evil.

Shakespeare seems particularly upset by bad smells. He liked roses, for even dead they smell sweet, but 'Lilies that fester smell far worse than weeds' (Sonnet 94).

GROUNDLINGS' GOSSIP

It has been said that Shakespeare was not christened until 26 April, probably three days after his birth, to avoid evil. Traditionally, St Mark's Day, 25 April, was unlucky and called 'Black Crosses' day, whereupon 'the crosses and altars were...hung with black, and (some reported) the spectral company of those destined to die that year stalked the churchyard'.

Plunder the plough!

Shakespeare probably drew inspiration from the 'Plough plays', a version of the mummers' plays of the late Middle Ages. Some of these are still acted today in parts of England. A Plough play was a short, violent, mimed drama involving a madman, Beelzebub, an old lady, a young lady and a variety of young men as her suitors.

1564 Italian instrument maker Andrea Amati designs and manufactures the violin in Cremona.

1593 Admiral Sir Richard Hawkins recommends drinking orange or lemon juice as a way of preventing scurvy in the Navy.

1600 Smugglers steal seven coffee bean seeds and take them to India, breaking the Arabian monopoly in coffee growing.

1564~1616

'If Muesli be the Food of Love...'

Famine, forked radishes and dishy women

Food plays an essential part in everyone's life, but for Shakespeare, it also signified a route to a person's character or ambitions. He used images of food and eating to represent many aspects of human emotions. Today we are familiar with such images, and this is largely because they have become part of our cultural heritage.

A light breakfast for Petruchio and friends before another day trying to tame the shrewish Kate (and if she doesn't get him, the cholesterol is sure to).

Taste and the palate are very important catalysts for metaphor. Although we read of great banquets, the Elizabethans actually had a very limited range of foods at their disposal on a day-to-day basis. Everything depended on the time of year and the season. Fruits and spices may have been imported, but they didn't travel much beyond London, and fish was generally restricted to the coastal and river areas. Walter Raleigh had only just brought the humble potato (and tobacco, bless 'im), and winter meant salt meat, and more salt meat, with perhaps a turnip for dessert. Then there was the weather. Between 1592 and 1595 there were some terrible storms and floods which hit harvests badly, and the consequent shortages provoked rioting. It was immediately after the most disastrous summer of 1594 that Shakespeare wrote: '...the winds...as in revenge, have suck'd up from the sea / Contagious fogs; which falling in the land, / Hath every pelting river made so proud, / That they have overcome their continents ...and the green corn / Hath rotted ere his youth attain'd a beard; / The fold stands empty in the drowned field, / And crows are fatted with the murrion flock' (A Midsummer Night's Dream).

Poperin envy

'Plum', 'salmon's tail', 'withered pear', 'nest of spicery', all appear as Shakespearean terms for the female genitals. Whereas 'carrot', 'root', 'potato-finger', 'poperin pear', represented the male member, the size of which is variously described as either 'three-inch fool' or 'yard' (depending on who told the story). But, as the saying goes, 'it's not the size of your poperin pear that matters'!

1604 In France, work begins to construct a canal linking the River Loire with the River Seine.

1610 Italian painter Caravaggio dies of malaria, having spent his last four years as a fugitive, wanted for killing a man in a brawl in Rome.

1615 Coin-in-the-slot vending machines, selling loose tobacco, are introduced into taverns in Britain.

'Here you are, dear, turnip al dente with a turnip surprise for afters.'

Night's Dream) – to describe overindulgence. There's Falstaff's description of Justice Shallow as being like a '*forked radish, with a head carved fantastically upon it with a knife*' (*Henry IV*). Antony calls Cleopatra a dish '*for the gods*', who '*makes hungry where most she satisfies*' – now that's sexy writing! But in later plays there is possibly some reference to his experience with richer food as he prospered in London, especially of poor digestion, '*You had musty victual, and he hath help to eat it: / He is a very valiant trencherman; he hath excellent stomach*' (*Much Ado About Nothing*).

Food images are everywhere in Shakespeare's plays and poems. In the earlier works he uses fairly obvious images – '*...a surfeit of the sweetest things / The deepest loathing to the stomach brings*' (*A Midsummer*

GROUNDLINGS' GOSSIP

Flatulence was as much fun in Shakespeare's day as now, and its sound, the 'raspberry', the most common expression of disapproval from groundlings (a custom that should be revived). The clown starts: 'Thereby hangs a tail'. 'Where?' asks the musician, 'Marry, sir', comes the reply, 'by many a wind-instrument that I know!'

Elizabeth Taylor as Cleopatra, 'a dish for the gods who makes hungry where she most satisfies'.

123

1735 Painter William Hogarth completes his series of engravings entitled *The Rake's Progress*.

1750 English pornographic novelist John Cleland writes *Fanny Hill, or the Memoirs of a Woman of Pleasure*, which becomes a classic of erotic literature for the next 250 years.

1753 The British Museum comes into being as London physician Sir Hans Sloane bequeaths the nation his library of 50,000 volumes, several thousand manuscripts, coins, curiosities and pictures.

1730~1900

'More Matter, with Less Art'

Crawling Hamlets and grinning cardinals

Bardolatry hasn't been confined to theatre and literature. The works have also been represented in an enormous amount of painting, especially during the 18th and 19th centuries. At one point it was calculated that the number of pictures inspired by or drawn from Shakespeare's plays amounted to one-fifth of the total number of British literary paintings executed from about 1750 to 1900!

Hamlet ignores the play and keeps his eye on Claudius in Daniel Maclise's painting.

(1842), which shows Hamlet lying twisted on the floor, watching Claudius. Charles Kean's production of *Hamlet* in 1856 actually reproduced this scene on stage! It is thought that the first model for Hamlet creeping around on the ground was Kean's father, Edmund, in 1814. Macready did it too, in 1823. It reappeared via Edwin Booth in 1870, and Henry Irving in 1874. Last, but never least, Richard Burton did it in 1953!

Before the 20th century, the relationship between the arts was more interconnected. Actors and painters were credited with as much ability to interpret art as were critics. The growth in printing, engraving, book illustrations and postcards promoted the popularity of paintings derived from literary subjects. These 'history paintings', as they were known (despite depicting fictional situations and characters) popularized Shakespeare's plays and even influenced actors and producers. One famous example is Daniel Maclise's *The Play Scene in Hamlet*

Get me out of here!

Seemingly one of the worst pictures of a Shakespeare scene was George Romney's *The Tempest* (1790), which depicts the moment of the shipwreck. The sea is hopelessly unrealistic, the figures are wooden, Miranda is looking the wrong way and Prospero is staring upwards to the top of the painting as if he wants someone to lower a rope and take him away!

1756 The Duc de Richelieu, a bon vivant who sometimes invites his guests to dine in the nude, invents mayonnaise, a mixture of egg yolks, vinegar or lemon juice, oil and seasonings.

1871 The Bank Holiday Act is passed in Britain, and the first bank holiday takes place in August of that year.

1876 Henrik Ibsen's play *Peer Gynt* is produced at Oslo's Christiania Theater, with a *Peer Gynt Suite* by Edvard Grieg.

Among the most famous artists who 'illustrated' the Bard were William Hogarth (1697–1764) with *A Scene from The Tempest* (1730–35). William Blake (1757–1827) also painted many including *Lear and Cordelia in Prison* (1778–80), *Oberon, Titania and Puck* (1785) and even *A Portrait of Shakespeare* (1800–1803) – difficult since he'd been dead for almost 200 years. Sir Joshua Reynolds (1723–92) painted an image of *Cardinal Beaufort's Bedchamber* (1780s) said to be taken from *Henry VI, Part Two*, when Warwick observed, 'See how the pangs of death do make him grin'. In the picture the

> ### GROUNDLINGS' GOSSIP
>
> Perhaps the most famous painting of any of Shakespeare's characters is *Ophelia* (1851–52) by Sir John Everett Millais. But it wasn't liked at the time. He was accused of suffocating her in 'vegetable anomalies'. But Millais had studied botany thoroughly before executing the work, and included 'poppies for sleep' and violets for 'death in youth'. One unimpressed critic didn't like her 'mouth...somewhat gaping'.

Cardinal is indeed grinning hugely – probably over his part in Gloucester's death. Later artists practising Bardistry were Dante Gabriel Rossetti (1828–82), with *Hamlet and Ophelia* (1858), *The First Madness of Ophelia* (1864), and *Study for the Death of Lady Macbeth* (1875), and Ford Madox Brown (1821–93), who produced *The Lear Drawings* (1843–44), *Romeo and Juliet* (1867) and, of course, a painting of Henry Irving's 1892 production of *King Lear*.

Millais's *Ophelia* (1851–52) hangs in the Tate Gallery, London, complete with authentic vegetation.

c. 222 Chinese alchemists of the Wu dynasty invent gunpowder by mixing sulphur and saltpetre at the correct temperature to produce an explosive.

c. 698 The Lindisfarne Gospels are written and illuminated.

1040 Scotland's young Duncan Canmore is slain by his nobles, who invite the king of Inverness, Macbeth (or Malebaethe), Mormaor of Moray, to succeed. Macbeth will reign until 1057.

200~1600

Haemorrhoids? Blame it on Uranus
Of astronomy, celestial orbs and disease

When Cleopatra cries out 'O sun, Burn the great sphere thou movest in', she is referring to the (even then) old-fashioned idea that the sun revolved around the earth (which it doesn't, apparently). But if she'd cried 'O sun, Burn the really small planet that moves around thee in an elliptical orbit', it wouldn't have been quite the same.

Cleo looking like she might do a bit of burning herself.

Although Shakespeare kept up with the latest from that new Italian kid, Nicolaus Copernicus, he was reluctant to give up the old images because they provided him with stunning metaphors for human feelings and actions in relation to the scale of the universe. His works contain about 80 references to the sun, 50 to the stars, but only about 10 to the moon – one of my favourites being Hippolyta impatiently wishing her marriage date (the new moon) would come, *'Four days will quickly steep*

'Four nights will quickly dream away, and on the fifth I'm washing my hair.'

themselves in night; / Four nights will quickly dream away the time; / And then the moon, like to a silver bow / New-bent in heaven, shall behold the night / Of our solemnities.' (A Midsummer Night's Dream) Ahhh, sweet, isn't it?

Copernicus set out to try and improve on Ptolemy's idea that the heavens spun around the earth – an idea with some inaccuracies (like, er, being wrong) – until he observed that things were the other way round. Unfortunately the Church had put all their money on Ptolemy, so didn't agree and threatened to kill him. Galileo also fell foul of the church when he

126

1372 The Vatican asks an astronomer to correct the Julian calendar, in use since 46 BC, because it is too long by 11 minutes and 15 seconds each year, but the astronomer dies before he can make these changes.

1488 Portuguese master mariner Barolomeu Diaz sails around the south of Africa and places a stone pillar on a headland that becomes known as the Cape of Good Hope.

1589 Christopher Marlowe's play *The Famous Tragedy of the Rich Jew of Malta* premieres.

observed the four moons of Jupiter. He was made to recant – but he had his fingers crossed behind his back, so it didn't matter. But science apart, the 'spheres' in Shakespeare's day were far more than pretty lights in the sky. Elizabethans looked to the cosmos to solve all sorts of problems. Even the gathering of medicinal herbs was carried out in accordance with the movements of celestial orbs. Planetary 'forces', along with astrology and the supernatural, were used to diagnose and treat diseases. For example, the conjunction of Mars and Saturn was believed to have caused the plagues that hit England during Shakespeare's life. Eclipses were the worst; people thought they caused natural disasters and possibly death. As Gloucester cries to Edmund in *King Lear*, '*These late eclipses in the sun and moon portend no good to us...love cools, friendship falls off, brothers divide.*'

Who nose why?

Tycho Brahe, a Danish astronomer, had a most curious nose. While at university, and just like a student of today, he got into a drunken fight and lost part of it. Being a scientific fellow, not able to afford a good plastic surgeon and with no sense of style, he rebuilt his appendage with wax, gold and silver!

Mr Brahe fortunately looked further than his mangled nose and discovered a supernova in the constellation of Cassiopeia.

Copernicus's view of the universe showing people sitting in deep space.

1454 Johannes Gutenberg establishes the first large-scale printing workshop at Mainz and produces an edition of the Bible using movable type.

c.1500 Glass-makers in Venice introduce clear crystal glass.

c.1519 Spaniard Francisco Pizarro captures Incan ruler Atahualpa, accepts a ransom of around 30 million dollars in gold and silver, and then garrottes him anyway.

1450~1700

Double, Double, Toil and Trouble
Witchcraft, carnality and flibberdigibbets

During Shakespeare's lifetime, there was a strong belief in witchcraft and the supernatural, and witch-hunts were a common, if not too popular, sport. Shakespeare was a man of his time, and used images of such phenomena regularly. And he was in distinguished company. James I wrote Demonologie, *three volumes outlining his beliefs, which Shakespeare apparently used for the witches in* Macbeth.

Shakespeare used superstition and supernatural belief to serve dramatic functions, especially in *King Lear*. For example, Lear curses all his daughters and by the end of the play... well, they're all dead! Again, though the storm in *King Lear* is real, it also mirrors his inner turmoil. It begins after he vows vengeance on his daughters '*No, you unnatural hags, I will have such revenges on you both ... / ... they shall be / The terrors of the earth*'. The storm comes and rages on land and in his head '*...this tempest in my mind / Doth from my senses take all feeling else / Save what beats there*'. When Edgar and Lear meet on the heath, and Gloucester appears, Edgar cries, '*This is the foul fiend*

GROUNDLINGS' GOSSIP

Bethlehem Royal Hospital, founded in 1247, became England's first asylum for the mentally ill in 1403. Henry VIII gave administration of the Bethlehem hospital to London in 1547 and eventually it became known as 'Bedlam'. Thus the generic term for anyone suffering mental illness was 'Tom O'Bedlams', which is what Edgar called himself in *King Lear*.

1543 Copernicus defies the Church by stating that the planets go round the sun.

1692 Hundreds of innocent people are falsely accused of witchcraft during the Puritan-led witch-hunt in Salem, Massachusetts.

1700 *The Way of the World* by William Congreve is performed at the Lincoln's Inn Fields Theatre, London.

Fair is foul and foul is fair, / Hover through the fog and filthy air.' The RSC's witches in its 1986 *Macbeth*.

DRAMATIS PERSONAE

Shakespeare made Edgar's dialogue capture a fine line in crazy talk. He had him say the sort of things that are a wee bit of a give-away, such as, 'Pillicock sat on Pillicock-hill: Halloo, halloo, loo, loo!' and 'Bless thy five wits! Tom's a-cold, / O, do de, do de, do de. Do poor Tom some charity'. Yes, someone, please do! But he is the only character to offer Lear wise advice on his pitiful state: there's method in his madness.

Flibberdigibbet. / He begins at curfew and walks till the first cock. / He ... makes the harelip, / mildews the white wheat, and hurts the poor creature of earth. / ...Bid her alight and her troth plight / And aroint thee, witch, aroint thee!'

Witches were women, partly because they were regarded (by men) as morally weaker than men, thus easier for the devil to tempt. Also, they had insatiable carnal lust – apparently – which, as sweating clerics told each other (late at night, under those lovely rough sheets) is *Conclusive Proof* of witchcraft! Witches were either white witches or devil worshippers (more likely to be called *heretics*). Either kind could practise white magic (good) or black magic (bad). White witches didn't get burned so often, so it was the more popular career path.

Midwives were often accused of witchcraft *because they produced babies from other women's bodies*, which to the worldly clerics was more *proof!* If some poor woman was accused, she was tortured until she confessed, and then killed. Or, she could confess straight away, in which case she was just killed. Sounds fair to me.

As they say, it's a windy witch that blows no Mac any good.

1113 Novgorod's Church of St Nicholas pioneers the onion-domed style of Greek Orthodox church architecture.

1303 The universities of Avignon and Rome are founded.

1405 Timur the Lame (Tamburlaine), Uzbekistan's national hero and 'Conqueror of the World' (who later inspires Marlowe's epic drama) dies aged 69, 'foaming like a camel'.

1100~1850

Trust me, I'm a Doctor...
(and I've got just the cure for that!)

In King Lear, *Kent won't even allow the doctor to enter the sick chamber, reflecting a most prevalent attitude. Historically, medicine used to be a potentially dangerous career. If someone claimed to be a 'doctor', then couldn't cure the patient, they ran the risk of death. This is why doctors, when in doubt, sometimes invent fantastical reasons why a patient is ill, so making it someone else's (often the* patient's*) fault if they shuffle off their mortal coil!*

Lear checks Cordelia for signs of life while waiting for the doctor to finish his rounds on the golf course.

Shakespeare almost always depicts doctors as incompetent. True, there was much experimentation to extend knowledge in his time, but without anaesthetic it usually involved lots of alcohol, sharp blades and strong stomachs! Cures were still largely based on superstition and magic.

Basically it was believed that four 'humours', emanating from the liver, made up the human physiology. Thus a person might be melancholic, sanguine, choleric or phlegmatic, to different degrees. These humours were linked to the astrological charts thus: Cancer, Scorpio and Pisces (melancholic); Gemini, Libra and Aquarius (sanguine); Aries, Leo, Sagittarius (choleric); and Taurus, Virgo and Capricorn (phlegmatic). Humours were based on four body fluids, blood, yellow bile, black bile and phlegm, and these determined a person's physical or mental health. The logic behind this was that each fluid gave off vapours that

c.1480 Handpainted wallpaper appears for the first time in France.

1500 A Swiss vet successfully performs a caesarian section on his wife.

1742 Handel's *Messiah* receives its world premiere in Dublin.

A physician mixes up a batch of anything he can find (Trophine Bisot, 1595).

Doctor Death

In 1511 the English Parliament stated 'that no person within the city of London... may take upon him to exercise and occupy as a physician or Surgeon unless he be first examined, approved and admitted by the Bishop of London'. But 30 years later 'any person having knowledge of herbs, roots, and waters' was allowed to call themselves 'doctor'.

ascend to the brain (hence an 'attack' of the vapours). A dominant presence of blood meant a happy disposition, of yellow bile meant violence. Too much phlegm and one was cowardly, and an excess of black bile meant laziness. An imbalance in all of them caused melancholy.

One by-product of melancholy was hysteria (*Hysterica passio*, which meant 'fit of the mother'). Shakespeare's own daughter, Susanna, suffered from it. Embarrassingly, so did poor old King Lear: '*O! how this mother swells upward toward my heart! / Hysterica passio! down, thou climbing sorrow! / Thy elements below*'. This means his problem is feminine (now there's progressive for you). From the early Middle Ages to the 19th century, women were thought to suffer from a 'disease' of the womb (*hyster*) which induced choking,

partial paralysis, convulsions and lethargy. It was 'caused' by either a lack of sexual intercourse or retention of menstrual blood! And since it was used as a good metaphor for women being weaker than men were, this 'disease' justified the patriarchal control of women. The best remedy for this condition was considered, unsurprisingly, to be marriage.

GROUNDLINGS' GOSSIP

Shakespeare often refers to the three main organs of heart, liver and brain. The liver was the seat of the natural spirits and the origin of blood, which was considered to be agitated by the heart, and was the centre of life and of feelings. The brain was the source of reason, memory, imagination, and the home of the 'rational soul'.

1968 A CBS documentary *Hunger in America* describes the extent of deficiency diseases in the world's most affluent nation.

1969 Neil Armstrong and Buzz Aldrin tell mission control at Houston that 'the Eagle has landed' as they step on the Moon for the first time.

1976 Nicolas Roeg's film *The Man Who Fell to Earth*, starring glam-rock star David Bowie, is released.

1968~Stardate 2817.6
'Beam me up, Macduff!'
Where no Bard has gone before

'You can't appreciate Shakespeare until you've read him in the original Klingon' says General Chang in Star Trek VI. *Which means all those scholars here on earth who have been studying his writing for years have been completely wasting their time!*

The gloomy Dane, Klingon-style.

The wonderful television series and films of *Star Trek* are full of references to the Bard's work, and many Bardologists started off as Trekkies. Many episodes either draw directly on Shakespeare's plots and characters, or quote him, often mixing several of his works in one script! *The Conscience of the King* borrows its title and plot from *Hamlet* (even the troupe of 'players' appear, whose production of *Hamlet* Captain Kirk uses to reveal the guilt of a murderer). Just in case anyone doesn't like *Hamlet*, this episode also contains whole chunks of action and dialogue inspired by *Macbeth*, as does *Catspaw*; then there's the *Dagger of the Mind*, and some lovely lines from *The Tempest* in *Plato's Stepchildren*. *The Undiscovered Country* is, as its title confirms, also from *Hamlet*, and contains the departing Chang saying *'Parting is such sweet sorrow'*. During the last fight he utters *'Once more into the breach, dear friends'* (*Henry V*). Best of all, though, is *'Hath not a*

Sitting pretty, the cast of *Star Trek: The Next Generation.*

1981 Sony Walkman begins the fashion for personal stereos.

1984 Smart bombs, missiles guided by laser signals to hit their targets accurately, are developed.

1999 American schoolgirl Britney Spears tops the charts and sparks a trend for teen-girl popstars.

Klingon hands, organs . . . affections, passions? Tickle us, do we not laugh? Prick us, do we not bleed?' (The Merchant of Venice)!

My personal favourites come from *Star Trek: The Next Generation*. In *Encounter at Farpoint* Commander Picard says, 'Kill all the lawyers! The first thing we do, let's kill all the lawyers' (Henry VI). In *The Naked Now*, Data, a robot, says, 'When you prick me, do I not…leak?' (The Merchant of Venice)! In *Hide and Q*, Q says, 'All the galaxy's a stage', but Picard corrects him, 'World, not galaxy, all the world's a stage'. And he should know, because Patrick Stewart, who plays him, has worked for years with the Royal Shakespeare Company!

But this is not all. *The Klingon Language Institute*, founded in America in 1992 and patronized among others by academics (there's a surprise!), has, as one of its projects, the restoration of the complete works of

William Shatner as James T. Kirk, valiant captain of the Starship Enterprise.

Shakespeare to the 'original Klingon'. One of its 'proudest accomplishments' has been the publication of *Hamlet, Prince of Denmark (The Restored Klingon Version)* in March 1996. They hope to add translations of *Much Ado About Nothing* and *Macbeth*. I look forward to that. Or should I say 'buy nqop' which means 'That's great news' (literally, 'The plates are full') in Klingon.

Aye Aye! It's Christopher Plummer as General Chang looking suitably villainous.

DRAMATIS PERSONAE

In 1994 William Shatner (who started out doing the Bard at Stratford, Ontario) was a guest at a Star Trek convention. He was doing very well until he clearly became exasperated with the sort of questions he was getting from the fans. 'I'd just like to say,' he shouted, 'Get a life, will you, people! I mean, for crying out loud, it was just a TV show!' I'm sure that William Shakespeare would have much the same to say to similarly trivia-obsessed Bardologists.

1992 British-born Tina Brown, former editor of *Vanity Fair*, takes over as editor of *The New Yorker*.

1993 Mobile phones have become a common sight in most major cities throughout the world.

1994 British director Mike Newell's low-budget film *Four Weddings and a Funeral* sparks an interest in Auden's poetry after 'Stop All the Clocks' is read in the funeral scene.

1980~the future

To Cyberspace and Beyond!

Surfin' Shakespeare on the Net

If you type the word 'Shakespeare' into a large Internet web search engine, you will get something approaching half a million web pages listed! Admittedly this will include a few responses which may refer to 'Ron Shakespeare's Get'em Bright Bag-wash' – but it is still an overwhelming presence!

The Internet has only been around for about 23 years (and the World Wide Web for 13), yet in that time the number of people using it has multiplied beyond belief and this situation will undoubtedly continue until it is used as casually as electricity. All of Shakespeare's words, plays, poems and sonnets can be found there, duplicated over and over by way of commercial, academic, personal and related sites (there are plenty of 'Shakespeare Net nerds' out there).

Everyone who's anyone has a site! The Royal Shakespeare Company, the Shakespeare Birthplace

> **Bard's Bible**
> There is 'proof' in cyberspace that Shakespeare translated the King James Version of the Bible! In April, 1611, when the Bible was first published, Shakespeare was 46 years old (true). If you turn to Psalm 46, you'll see that the 46th word is 'shake' (true). Count back 46 words from the end of the Psalm and the last word is 'spear'! (True. Sad? Who's sad?)

The Bard goes online with the Royal Shakespeare Company's website.

For Bard facts and memorabilia, there's really only one place to look.

Trust, all (I think) of the Festival Theatres in America, England and Canada at least; the new Globe playhouse in London, as well as that lil' old Globe in Texas. And there are sites from all the continents of the world.

Of the best ones (and there are too many to mention them all here), 'The Works of the Bard' informs the surfer that it is the 'oldest Shakespeare site' on the Web and has had 'over 8 million hits since 1993'. Typically, it contains the entire works available scene by scene, by character personnel, by line quote and then has links to some of the other important sites, which then have links to others, etc. etc. 'The Collected Works of Shakespeare' gives 30 other links, including the excellent 'Mr William Shakespeare and the Internet'. Some sites are devoted to single plays, or characters (Hamlet is popular here) or themes. There's a site where you can generate your own Shakespearean-type insults! There are 'virtual classrooms' compiled by universities and schools for anyone to look at. Others continue the debate about authorship of his plays – they're *really* interesting – if there's no wet paint to watch.

How prophetic that Shakespeare's first main theatre was called the Globe. Today, over 400 years later, any of his plays can theoretically be read (and soon be seen no doubt) simultaneously by almost the entire population of the earth.

GROUNDLINGS' GOSSIP

In April 2000, the Shakespeare Birthplace Trust, together with the Shakespeare Centre, launched a global youth performance festival as part of the annual Shakespeare birthday celebrations. This allows young people between the ages of 11 and 30 to create multimedia performances of the Bard's work using anything from the radio to the Internet to reach audiences!

Endpiece

One form of Willy's wit that rarely appears in print because it is neither drama, nor poetry, nor sonnet, is the epitaph, of which he is supposed to have written several. Some of these were jokes, some serious, and though there is some evidence for them being written by him, there's not much, so they have an anecdotal quality about them.

One example of the more touching kind is on the tomb of Thomas Stanley, Knight and son of the Earl of Derby. Or rather, there are two inscriptions – one at each end. At the East End is the following verse:

> Ask not who lies here, but do not weep;
> He is not dead, he doth but sleep.
> This stony register is for his bones,
> His fame is more perpetual than these stones;
> And his own goodness, with himself being gone,
> Shall live when earthly monument is none.

And at the West End is written:

> Not monumental stone preserves our fame,
> Nor sky-aspiring pyramids our name;
> The memory of him for whom this stands
> Shall outlive marble and defacers' hands:
> When all to Time's consumption shall be given,
> Stanley, for whom this stands, shall stand in
>   heaven.

A pensive Joseph Fiennes in his 1999 starring role in *Shakespeare in Love*, which benefited from a witty script by the English playwright Tom Stoppard.

But no one knows whether these verses are for the same person, or even which 'Stanley' it was.

Shakespeare is also supposed to have written an epitaph for the brewer, Elias James of Puddle Wharf (very close to the Blackfriars Theatre – so beer was probably piped backstage). It's a bit dull, to be honest, and makes the brewer out to be a rather 'godly' person (now that's a first!).

> When God was
>   pleas'd (the world
>   unwilling yet),
> Elias James to nature
>   paid his debt,
> And here reposeth; as
>   he liv'd and died,
> The saying in him
>   strongly verified,
> 'Such life, such death.'
>   Then, the truth
>   known to tell,
> He liv'd a godly life,
>   and died as well.

This has caused many to deny that it was written by Shakespeare, though recent research has shown it probably was. Another one, reported by both Nicholas Burgh, a Knight of Windsor, and Thomas Plume, the Archdeacon of Rochester, has Shakespeare and Jonson in an inn playing word games with each other's epitaphs. There seems to be no record of what Jonson wrote for Shakespeare, but after he began his own, 'Here lies Ben Jonson, who once was one...' Shakespeare took up a pen and wrote, *'Here lies Benjamin with short hair upon his chin, / Who while he lived was a slow thing; and now he's / buried is no thing'.* This comments rather cuttingly upon Jonson's well-known slowness of manner.

The best-known epitaph ascribed to the Bard is for John A. Combe, who sold him land in 1602. Combe was a moneylender, whose interest rate was 'ten in the hundred'.

> Ten in the hundred must lie in his grave,
> But a hundred to ten whether God will him have.
> Who then must be interr'd in this tomb?
> 'Oh', quoth the Devil, 'my John a Combe.'

It has also been claimed Shakespeare wrote another for John's brother, Tom Combe:

> Thin in beard, & thick in purse;
> Never man beloved worse:
> He went to th' grave with many a curse:
> The Devil & He both had one nurse.

Tongue in cheek, and a cheeky tongue.

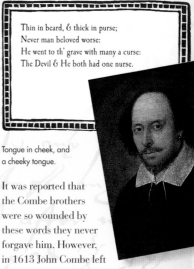

It was reported that the Combe brothers were so wounded by these words they never forgave him. However, in 1613 John Combe left Shakespeare £5 in his will, so he must have had a change of heart.

Jonson wasn't the only one to dedicate an epitaph to Shakespeare. Folio No. 26 (Folger collection) contains the following anonymous tribute:

'Here Shakespeare lies whom none but death could shake; / And here shall he judgement all awake;
When the last trumpet doth unclose his eyes, / The wittiest poet in the world shall rise.'

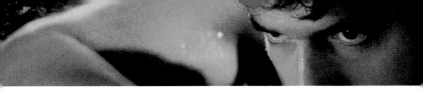

Glossary of Terms

Before you try to juggle with your bauble, or carve your wagtail, check this glossary. The vocabulary and slang may have been different in Shakespeare's day, but the preoccupations were much the same.

ARCHIVES
The place where public records are kept.

BARDOLATRY
The worship of all things Shakespearean.

BAUBLE
Slang for 'penis'.

BEARWARD
A man who keeps bears for baiting by dogs.

BEAST
Used to describe both men and gods (as in 'make the beast with two backs' – *Othello*). In reference to gods it means to behave like a sexually obsessed animal (man), and in man it means to have the sexual appetite of an animal.

BEDLAM
The Bethlehem Royal Hospital, founded in 1247, which became England's first asylum for the mentally ill in 1403. The generic term for anyone suffering mental illness was 'Tom O'Bedlams'.

BIRD'S NEST
Female pubic hair and genitals ('Must climb a bird's nest soon when it is dark' – *Romeo and Juliet*).

BOTTOM-GRASS
From that thick short grass which grows at the bottom of a meadow – a double-entendre for hair around the crotch and posterior.

BURGESS
An important citizen of a borough or a town.

CAPCASE
A small travelling case or bag.

CARVING
A woman's gesture of raising and wiggling the little finger when drinking from a vessel; used by prostitutes to signal availability.

CATAMITES
Boys procured by monks for sex.

CHRONICLE PLAY
A specific type of history play.

COOPER
A maker of barrels and casks, useful to the breweries.

DARK LADY

The mysterious woman for whom many of the sonnets were supposedly written. It is thought she was Mary Fritton, Maid of Honour at Court.

DIE

Elizabethan slang for having an orgasm.

DISGUISING

A favourite pastime of courtiers within pageants and masques. It allowed flirtation protected by anonymity *(see Master of Revels, page 44)*.

DOUBLET

A man's jacket, usually tight at the waist, and with separate baggy sleeves tied on with points.

FARTHINGALE

A stiff umbrella frame of bone worn under women's skirts to give a wide shape to the dress.

FLETCHER

A maker of arrows.

FOLIO

A sheet of paper folded once to make two 'leaves' or four pages or sides. Books made this size were also called folios – hence the First Folio (1623).

FOUL PAPERS

An outline plot of a play fought over by actors, producers and stage managers.

GROUNDLINGS

Those who stood to watch a performance in a theatre and paid the least money.

HEAD-TIRE

A head-dress, usually specially made for a particular occasion.

HUMOURS

The four body fluids, emanating from the liver – blood, yellow bile, black bile and phlegm – which were believed to determine a person's physical or mental health. And who's to say they weren't correct?

HYSTERICA PASSIO

The 'fit of the mother', and a by-product of melancholy, supposedly 'caused' by a lack of sexual intercourse or a retention of menstrual blood. Cured by an enthusiastic juggling session.

IAMBIC PENTAMETER

A poetic rhythm of ten or eleven syllables in pairs with emphasis placed on the second syllable of each pairing.

JEWEL

Colloquial word for virginity or chastity ('to take from you the jewel you hold so dear' – *Pericles*).

JUGGLE

A euphemism for sexual intercourse: drawn from 'jugglers' balls' as testicles.

'KNOG HIS URINALS'

To knot someone's testicles. A comic threat to dismember someone's marital apparatus. Similar to having their 'guts for garters'.

LIVERY
Special dress or uniform. Each nobleman would have his own livery in which he dressed those in his employ.

LORD OF MISRULE
Someone elected during the winter festivities to 'preside' over the bad behaviour of, mainly, students and apprentices. Also known as Christmas Lord.

LOST YEARS
The period between 1585 and 1592 for which there are no records of Shakespeare's whereabouts or activities – though various salacious rumours have been recorded.

MALADY OF FRANCE
A term for syphilis, since it originally came to England from France.

MANDRAKE
('Thou whoreson mandrake' – *Henry IV*): a narcotic herbaceous plant, which is supposed to shriek when pulled up. The mandrake is associated with evil and has certain other properties: for example when men are hanged they allegedly ejaculate, and if such emissions hit the ground, it is thought the mandrake will grow.

MASQUE
A private entertainment consisting of an allegorical or mythological theme, poetry, music, dance, masks, elaborate costumes and stage machines.

MASTER OF THE REVELS
Court version of the Lord of Misrule – responsible for choosing plays and actors.

MEDLAR
Shakespeare uses this word to describe the crotch area. It also alludes to the female pudenda.

MORRIS DANCING
A form of traditional dance dating back to the Middle Ages or earlier, in which bells and handkerchiefs are worn, and involving mock fights with sticks.

MYSTERY PLAY
A medieval play based on Bible stories. The word comes from an archaic term for a trade.

NUNNERY

(As in 'get thee to a nunnery' – *Hamlet*) not only meant a convent but also intended as a pun on 'nunnery' as the Elizabethan slang word for brothel.

PARING KNIFE
A glover's tool, referred to by Shakespeare, for cutting leather.

POINTS
Laces for fastening clothes together.

PROPERTIES
Props, or any item of furniture used in a play.

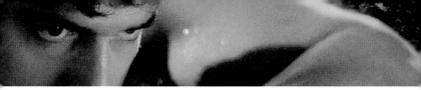

PUCELLE
'Maid' or 'virgin' in medieval French.

PUZZEL
'Whore' in Elizabethan slang.

QUARTO
A sheet of paper folded twice to make four leaves, thus eight pages or sides (half the size of a folio).

RUFF
Normally the frill which goes round the neck on a woman's dress, it was also slang for the female genitals and was thus close to 'muff'.

SHAKESPEAREAN SONNET
A verse of complete idea, composed of 14 rhymed iambic pentameter lines arranged in the pattern abab, cdcd, efef, gg, where each letter stands for a line and all lines with the same letter are supposed to rhyme.

STRUMPET
A whore, prostitute, woman of absolutely no morals whatsoever ('O most unhappy strumpet' – *Hamlet*).

TIRE
To dress, from 'attire'. Also means equipment or costume generally.

TIRING-HOUSE
A place for actors to change clothes before a play. Built behind the stage in the public playhouses. More recently known as the 'green room'.

TITHE
A tax, being a tenth part of a person's goods or even animals.

VORTIGERN
A play supposedly written by Shakespeare, but really the work of forger William Henry Ireland. It was produced at Drury Lane in 1796, with Kemble in the lead role, and laughed off stage.

WAGTAIL
Not the bird, but a loose and lascivious woman. Also occasionally used to describe a womanizing man.

WHALE TO VIRGINITY
(Like a, as in 'I knew this young count who is a whale to virginity, and devours up all the fry it finds' – *All's Well That Ends Well*) – an enthusiastic womanizer, who knows no restraint.

WHITTAWER
A maker of fine leather goods, such as gloves, but also saddles, etc.

WITTOL
When a man accommodates his wife's adultery through either his weakness or for other reasons, such as to justify his own wandering.

Index

PHOTOGRAPHIC CREDITS

The publishers are grateful to the following for permission to reproduce copyright material. Every effort has been made to trace copyright holders and the publishers would be grateful to be informed of any errors or omissions for correction in future editions.

AKG, London: 16t (Victoria & Albert Museum, London), 43, 78/79 (Staatliche Kunstsammlungen, Kassel)

The Art Archive, London: 86, 125

The Art Archive/Garrick Club: 23, 47b, 55m, 66, 88t, 88b, 108, 110/111, 115b

Bridgeman Art Library, London: 15 (Guildhall Library, London), 17, 22b, 28, 30, 34, 52 (Victoria & Albert Museum, London), 55r (Royal Holloway and Bedford New College, London), 58/59 (Townley Hall Art Gallery and Museum), 60/61 (Museo d'Arte Moderno di Ca Pesaro), 63t (Royal Pavilion Museum, Brighton), 77 (National Gallery of Victoria and Melbourne), 80 (Boughton House), 83 (Rafael Valls Gallery), 84 (Bolton Museum Art Gallery), 87b (Walker Art Gallery, Liverpool), 91 (Guildhall Art Gallery, London), 124 (Roy Miles Gallery), 131 (Ashmolean Museum, Oxford)

Roger Viollet/BAL: 36 (Musée Saint-Denis, Rheims)

Cameron Collection: 25, 40, 48, 73t, 75, 120, 123, 130

Corbis, London: 73b, 74 + 76 + 97t (Robbie Jack), 92 (J. Gurney), 93, 95t

Corbis/Bettmann: 102m, 104, 110

Photographs Courtesy The Kobal Collection, London: 8 (Olivier Prods/London Films/Big Ben Films), 29 + 136, 81b 109 (Miramax Films/Universal Productions), 32/33 (Working Title /BBC/BR Screen), 48/49, 61 + 103b (Rolf Konow/Castle Rock/Dakota Films), 64 (Mirisch–7 Arts/United Artists), 94, 95m, 98 (Films Marceau/Mercury Prods), 99t (MGM), 98/99 (20th Century-Fox), 100 (Universal), 101t (Boyd's Co), 102t (United Artists), 106t (TOHO), 106b (Herald Ace-Nippon-Herald-Greenwich), 107t (Art Film AB), 107B (Mosfilm), 115, 122 (Columbia), 126 (Film 4/Arts Council/Capitol), 133 (Paramount)

The Performing Arts Library, London: 27 (Pete Jones), 33 + 67 + 74 (Fritz Curzon), 37 + 47t (Henrietta Butler), 45 (Michael Ward), 65m (Ben Christopher), 67 (Mark Douet)

PAL/Clive Barda: 49, 63b, 116, 117, 120, 126r, 128/129

Rex Features, London: 53, 27, 38, 53, 68, 70, 85, 97b, 101b, 111, 113r, 121

Other images from Private Collections